Portfolio Assessment in the Reading-Writing Classroom

Robert J. Tierney

Mark A. Carter

Laura E. Desai

Illustrations: Susan Myers

Editorial Assistance: Carolyn Cutler

Christopher-Gordon Publishers, Inc. Norwood, MA

Credit Lines

Student handout on portfolios, portfolio peer review sheet and excerpt from report on Apple Classroom of Tomorrow used with permission of Sheila Cantlebary and Richard Tracy.

Materials from student writing portfolio (student questions for self-evaluation of portfolio writing, conference for portfolio assessment, possible criteria for assessment and supplementary report to parents used with the permission of the Office of Teaching and Learning, Columbus, Ohio, City Schools.

Letters to parents used with permission of Darice Fritschle, second grade teacher, Bay Village, Ohio, and Jan Beagle, Barrington Elementary School, Barrington, Ohio.

Integrated language instruction checklist, matrix of performance criteria entries one and two, and characterizing the portfolio entry one used with permission of Stanford Teacher Assessment Program.

Peer/teacher response to portfolios used with permission of Rebecca Camp, Educational Testing Service.

Material on criteria for individual portfolios, criteria for program, and summary of Vermont statewide writing assessment used with permission of the Department of Education, State of Vermont.

"Students subvert own test scores," article from *The New York Times*, May 3, 1989, used with permission.

Copyright © 1991 by *Christopher-Gordon Publishers, Inc.*

ISBN: O-926842-08-0

10 9 8 7 6   96 95 94 93 92

Table of Contents

Preface

The purpose of this book is to give teachers some ideas about how they can implement portfolios in their classrooms. It contains reproductions of actual materials used by teachers in classrooms (e.g., copies of letters sent to parents, handouts to students, checklists, and so forth) as well as examples of student portfolios across subjects and grades. It also provides research-based information to help teachers explain portfolio concepts to parents, the community, administrators, and other interested parties.

The book repeatedly emphasizes that there is no "right" way to implement portfolios, that each classroom will reflect a unique approach to authentic assessment, and that each child's collection of documents will differ. To this end, we have attempted to provide many examples from all the different classrooms in which we have been, and we have tried to illustrate the many ways teachers have used portfolios from kindergarten through high school.

The most important idea we wish to convey is the spirit of portfolios: developing classroom practices and traditions that reflect a student-centered approach to assessment.

Five basic beliefs are at the root of the ideas in this book:

1. Teachers are capable professionals who have the capacity to facilitate intellectual and emotional growth in students. With teaching comes a commitment to a lifelong educational process for both the teachers and their students. When teachers are given autonomy and respect, they can create classrooms with positive, supportive environments that foster excellence among students.

2. Students are learning how to think for themselves and how to educate themselves over the course of their lives. When given ownership over the direction of their learning, they will work to their greatest capacity and in a creative fashion.

3. Reading and writing are not only essential survival skills in this society but are also pathways for a lifelong educational process, for self-expression, and for socio-economic, political, and personal empowerment. The history of civilization has

been a history of ideas. The classroom is a microcosm where students can learn to engage with their own ideas as well as the ideas of others and can learn to communicate and use these ideas effectively.

4. Diversity is not only inevitable, it is also desirable. The process of education should reflect the diversity of human experience and creativity. Only through respect for diversity can excellence be achieved, since excellence involves people working to their ultimate capacity. If we attempt to define that capacity or make it uniform across students, we cut it off. If students are empowered to find that capacity for themselves, they will frequently surprise us with their abilities.

5. The key word in the relationship between teachers and students is respect, and this must be mutual. Respect cannot be based on the students' fear of punishment by teachers and the teachers' concomitant right to judge the personal worth of students. Rather, respect is characterized by an understanding that all human beings are worthy and what they create (whether it is a short story or a classroom) is also worthwhile. The education process seeks ways to expand people's ability to create and the range of their creations and to make their creations effective vehicles for learning, communication, and progress.

While this book names three coauthors, many others authored what is described in the book. The thoughts related to portfolios have been shaped in conjunction with a multiyear research and development effort with teachers, administrators, and others interested in portfolios.

In 1987, Rob Tierney was challenged by his friend and colleague, David Pearson, "to put up or shut up." Rob had been very critical of David's attempts to establish a new and better reading assessment for the state of Illinois. Rob's argument was that the test was not addressing some of the major problems with testing. He suggested to David that it was adding more problems. As he stated, "It's the emperor's new clothes. It is still a test by which outsiders define and measure literacy in an arbitrary and rather singular fashion." David's response, which was perhaps understandable, was, "I agree. But I would prefer that critics [such as yourself] either suggest alternatives or stop criticizing those of us who are trying to do so."

Over the next year or so, Rob struggled with the challenge. During this period, his work with Columbus City Schools had led to his development of primary trait assessment procedures as well as student directed self-assessment. At the same time, some of his Columbus City Schools colleagues suggested that portfolios might be worthwhile pursuing. Toward the end of 1987, Laurie Desai expressed an interest in assessment, and together Rob and Laurie began a search for information on portfolios. Over the fall of 1987, we gathered whatever information we could. In February 1988, Rob and Laurie (together with Mark Carter, who shared their interest) began working with seven volunteer teachers exploring their use of portfolios. Since 1988 they have researched portfolios in several school districts.

There are a number of dimensions to these pursuits. To develop assessment practices that allow for a more robust representation of students' work and serve to empower teacher and student learning, we (Mark Carter, Laurie Desai, and Rob Tierney, with the support of Antonia Moss) have been involved in studies examining the certain portfolio-related assessment practices.

1. We have been concerned with developing a model for using portfolios in the classroom—what reading and writing portfolios might include; how portfolios might be developed by students and teachers; what purposes portfolios might serve; how teachers and students might use portfolios along with ongoing assessment and learning. We have been concerned with how classrooms, schools, and school districts might implement portfolios.

2. We have developed a keen interest in self-assessment—in particular, student self-selection of past work, procedures that support self-reflection, and the establishment of ongoing learning goals.

3. We have been interested in exploring the impact of portfolios upon students and teachers as well as parents.

4. We are interested in what might be viewed as an obvious but disregarded issue: the assessment of assessment. Our goal is not to have a vested interest in portfolios *per se* but to pursue the assessment of assessment as we study the impact of a set of assessment procedures involving portfolios. At the beginning, our pursuit of this question in terms of teacher and student empowerment was unique.

A related goal has to do with sponsoring change in classrooms and developing procedures for implementing and studying the implementation of assessment procedures. Over the three years of the project, we have incorporated the use of a teacher-researcher model in which we have tried to follow the lead of teachers as they develop portfolio practices to fit their classrooms and as they have joined with us in researching portfolio use. In year one we pursued case studies of teachers who were interested in trying portfolios in their classrooms. In year two, we set up comparisons between teachers who did and those who did not use portfolios. In the third year, we approached the study of portfolios using a time-series approach that allowed us to compare teachers with themselves (prior to, during, and after the use of portfolios) as well as with teachers who began using portfolios at different times.

The project was truly a research and development effort. We began by reviewing existing literature on the uses of portfolio for assessment purposes. We found very little information on portfolios and no research. As we discussed portfolios with others we found several advocates of their use and occasional, alleged use. On exploring these claims, however, we found that they were where we were—their advocacy was stronger than their explication of how it might be implemented. In situations where portfolios were supposedly being used, a close examination suggested that the portfolios were more idle than dynamic. For example, such teachers did little more than have students accumulate work in folders. It was not until we began exploring the use of portfolios in other fields (e.g., art education) that we discovered any substantial discussion of their use.

As we immersed ourselves in thinking about portfolios, some definition of their possible uses began to emerge. We began to see portfolios as systematic collections by students and teachers that could help both consider effort, improvement, processes, and achievement across a diverse range of texts that were read or written. Critical features that began to emerge were an emphasis upon process and product and student involvement in self-assessment. It was this latter feature that we sensed was most often lacking from past conceptualizations of the use of portfolios.

What also emerged from our review were more questions than answers: How might portfolios be operationalized in different classrooms? What might portfolios that emphasized product look like? How might students be involved in managing portfolios? How might students begin to assess their own efforts? How successful would these self-assessments be? What impact might portfolios have upon teachers, especially teachers' views of their students? Above all, what impact might portfolios have upon the students? Would the students have a clearer and more positive view of themselves as readers and writers? Would they develop a more discerning understanding of their strengths, processes, and improvement?

Rather than speculate about the answers to these questions, we chose to pursue this project as a research and development effort in close collaboration with K-12 teachers. Working with the Columbus, Ohio City Schools, Westerville, Ohio Schools, and Upper Arlington, Ohio School District we were able to locate seven interested teachers to pursue the use of portfolios in their classrooms and help us answer some of our questions.

In working with the teachers we did not want to prescribe what they might do. We gave them broad guidelines and worked with them as they fashioned portfolios to fit their individual situations. We stressed the importance of using portfolios as a means of highlighting process along with product, the value of effort and improvement along with achievement, and the basis for engaging students in self-evaluation. To stimulate their thinking, we shared with them audiotaped interviews along with slides showing portfolio use by a high school artist and by a journalism student.

Over the course of the two years we worked with the teachers and their students as they explored the uses of portfolios. We obtained answers to some of our questions from observations. We sought other answers through interviews with selected students and the teacher. Four students of varying abilities and their teacher were interviewed periodically over the year. We held meetings with teachers outside of the classroom. In addition, we had comparison classrooms that were not using portfolios. We hoped that by the end of the year we would have the basis for offering educated advice rather than speculative suggestions on how others might use portfolios. We feel that our hopes were realized.

In the first and second years of the study we explored the issue of student and teacher empowerment. While a demonstration of the impact of portfolios was forthcoming, the data was not clearly comparative (i.e., we did not have a comparison with teachers who did not use portfolios) and was restricted to a relatively small sample. To afford a clearer comparative assessment across a large number of teachers and students, a more expansive detailed and careful comparison of the use of portfolios is being pursued.

The third year was devoted to pursuing such a study at the same time as we worked in an entire school district (Bay Village Schools). In terms of research design, the third year study represented an attempt (1) to integrate traditional comparisons (forced and random) with a time-series approach and (2) to implement a research design that would work in a school setting in which teachers need support rather than interference. Two sets of comparison were pursued. The first set involved a comparison across selected teachers and students who initiated portfolios at staggered times during the year. As depicted in

Figure 1, three randomly assigned cohorts, whose initiation of portfolios was staggered, were compared four different times.

Figure 1

	T_1			T_2			T_3			T_4
Cohort 1	o	x	x	o	x	x	o	x	x	o
(N=7)										
Cohort 2	o			o	x	x	o	x	x	o
(N=7)										
Cohort 3	o			o			o	x	x	o
(N=7)										

x denotes classroom use of portfolios
o denotes observations of teachers and students

T1 corresponds to beginning of quarter one
T2 corresponds to beginning of quarter two
T3 corresponds to beginning of quarter three
T4 corresponds to beginning of quarter four

The second set involved a comparison of the randomly assigned cohorts with a fixed nonportfolio group. As depicted in Figure 2, each of the three portfolio cohorts were compared with the nonportfolio group.

Figure 2

Comparison of cohorts with nonportfolio group

	T_1			T_2			T_3			T_4
Cohort 1	o	x	x	o	x	x	o	x	x	o
Cohort 2	o			o	x	x	o	x	x	o
Cohort 3	o			o			o	x	x	o
Nonportfolio	o			o			o			o

Twenty-two teachers from grades 3 through 7 constituted the portfolio group as well as twenty-nine teachers in the nonportfolio group. The twenty-two teachers were randomly assigned to the various portfolio cohorts; the nonportfolio cohort was fixed. Four students from each class were randomly selected to represent above average and below average ability groups. Furthermore, a subsample of parents of the students from each class was selected for questioning.

The teacher data, which was collected four times, includes transcribed interviews of self-reports and written analyses of the following:

1. Classroom assessment practices;
2. Classroom instructional practices;
3. Sources used to assess students;
4. Sources used to plan instruction;
5. Belief systems, background of experiences regarding reading and writing;
6. Analyses of interview questionnaires.

The students' data, which was collected four times, include transcribed interviews of students directed at determining:

1. Self-assessment of strengths and weaknesses;
2. Perceptions of how their reading and writing has changed;
3. Perceptions of how others judge their writing;

as well as (at the end of the year) selected samples of their work with comments and copies of the self-evaluation comments.

The parent data also includes their written responses to:

1. Their perceptions of their child's growth as a reader and writer;
2. Their perceptions of the information they are provided by the teachers in the various cohorts;
3. Their description of how they interact with their child as a reader/writer.

Simultaneously, other initiatives began in other sites. For example, Mark Carter pursued his doctoral thesis at Barrington Elementary in Upper Arlington, focusing on the development of student self-assessment. Laurie Desai and Rob Tierney explored the use of portfolios in a high school classroom where students were involved in learning within the context of technology-based classrooms.

As we look over these involvements, we recognize that this book could not have been written until now. It has taken time to learn about the portfolio process in the reading-writing classroom—what it is and what it is not. It has taken until now to recognize what to say to teachers about what we have learned about portfolios and share what the teachers, students, parents, and administrators have shared with us. We especially wish to thank those who encouraged us.

They include Carolyn Allen, Linda Allenbach, Terry Appell, Jackie Ashmun, Marie Ashmus, Brenda Behrendt, Patty Berkowitz, Evelyn Biesterfeldt, Terrie Botkins, Edwina Bradley, Carol Brown, Linda Cannon, Sheila Cantlebary, Chris Cassidy, Virginia Charles, Kay Coletta, Sharon Danison, Lisa Dapoz, Jackie Day, Sharon Dorsey, David Dwyer, Maggie Eaton, Moira Erwine, Martha Fisher, Darice Fritschle, Joan Fusco, Toby Gilliland, Nancy Glinka, Jean Hartman, Jayne Hertvik, MaryBeth Hoke, Jodi Jirik, Roz Kalinoski, Arlene Karnatz, Jill Kuhn, Lucy Laing, Maureen Larsen, Peggy Liberatore, Rita Loksa, Duanne MacMillan, Carol McCabe, Kelli McMaugh, Carol Neutzling, Julie Nuskin, Randy Rush, Marcia Schinski, Marion Shoemaker, Jean Sperling, Randy Stortz, Burlah Taylor, Shirley Thompson, Shirley Tillia, Richard Tracy, Arlene Way, and Barbara Woodburn.

In addition we offer special thanks to Susan Myers who did the illustrations; and Antonia Moss for her help in countless ways in the preparation of the book.

A final word: While we hope this book will prompt teachers to pursue portfolios in their classrooms, we know it will not provide answers to every question they might have. We would not want it to do so. Ideally, we would prefer that teachers proceed as if they were investigating the possibility of using portfolios for the first time. Since each setting is different and each student unique, the implementation of portfolios will be somewhat idiosyncratic.

If we approach portfolios with a research and development orientation, we simply ask ourselves to identify possible goals for portfolios and consider possible procedures and ways we can keep tabs on what is happening. Thus we are open to revamping our processes, reexamining possibilities, and exploring promising avenues.

Part One

Assessment
in the
Classroom

Chapter 1

Questions and Answers About Portfolios

In our experience with workshops on portfolios, teachers often have specific questions about implementing portfolios in their classrooms. In order to address these concerns, we arranged the interview/discussion below. Rob Tierney is a professor in the department of Educational Theory and Practice at Ohio State University. His specialties are Critical Thinking, Reading Comprehension, and Reading and Writing Research. Mark Carter has been an elementary school teacher for ten years and is currently serving as a "teacher on special assignment" in the Upper Arlington, Ohio, school district. He is completing a doctoral degree in education at Ohio State; his dissertation topic is a study of portfolios and self-assessment. Laurie Desai has taught in Duluth, Georgia. She is working on her doctorate at Ohio State University, where she is a research assistant with the Apple Classroom of Tomorrow[SM] program. Carolyn Cutler, who has worked closely with the three authors in the organization and revision of this text, moderated the interview. She is a graduate student at Ohio State in the Master of Liberal Studies program.

The "Spirit" of the Portfolio Classroom

Carolyn: The governing question seems to be the spirit of portfolios, the spirit of the classroom that you are trying to convey through the book. Why is it so important for students to have a sense of ownership? What does that mean for students to have ownership and what sort of classroom environment allows that ownership to take place?

Rob: The concept of portfolios is really driven by an attempt to actually approach the issue of assessment in a manner which befits different classrooms and different students. Our goal from the very outset was to have assessment which was responsive to what students were doing; assessment that represents the range of things they're involved in; the processes they enlisted, the effort they put in, and the improvement and the range of abilities that students have demonstrated.

We were concerned that traditional assessment was both limited and subversive. Students and their teachers' creative energies were being subverted into students being prepared to respond to tests which have very little relationship to literacy as we know it. We want to provide a rich literacy environment in which assessment is linked to what the child is doing and might do. In other words, there is some return from assessment—namely, the child is empowered.

Mark: Ultimately, we want students to grow to be independent. For them to do that, they have to have a sense of what the criteria is that makes them successful. For a long time, the criteria has been a mystery to students. Part of the spirit is inviting students to help develop the criteria so that they know exactly what they have to work toward to be successful.

A second aspect that I'm really concerned about is that students produce quality work. I think part of the spirit is that we want students to feel ownership and involvement so they have a stake in the work that they're producing; that they want it to be good. I think if we want students to produce quality work then we have to let students have a say in the kinds of work that they're going to be doing. If children are working from their own interests towards criteria that they think are understandable and reasonable for where they are, we have a much better chance of having children work at a level to produce the kinds of quality work that in many cases is absent in lots of classrooms. Portfolios are the link to help the students see the kinds of things that they're doing so that they can indeed make improvements over a period of time.

Laurie: And when they really care about what it is they're doing, then they care more about improving it, too. When it seems so totally isolated and removed from anything that matters to them, then they don't care.

Rob: Portfolios do provide something that even rich literacy classrooms did not have in place. In particular no matter what the literacy environment, whether it be literacy-based or whole language, it really didn't invite students to be part of the assessment. Portfolios actually get students involved in reflecting upon what it is they're about; what goals they have; what they're achieving and how they have improved.

The difficulty that anybody is going to have with portfolios is developing the pedagogy around them. There's a dearth of worthwhile pedagogical suggestions with respect to getting students involved in self-assessment. As we've been involved in portfolios we're learning what it means to get students involved in self-assessment.

Laurie: We're also giving teachers the opportunity for more self-assessment than they've had in the past. Portfolios allow the teacher to really look at what's going on in their classrooms in terms of the students' actual work instead of basing their judgment on standardized tests scores. We are suggesting a more valid method to determining the success of instructional methods.

Changing Role of the Teacher

Carolyn: Could you expand on the role of the teacher in portfolio classrooms?

Laurie: I think that while the teacher is the guiding force in any classroom, the teacher in a portfolio classroom is a part of the team and that the students are working with the teacher to establish goals. Of course they need someone there to help give the guiding direction, but the teacher is not the whole focus.

A lot of classes aren't student centered, they're teacher centered. The teacher is the focus of decisions, of what happens next, of what's considered good or bad, of what counts and doesn't count, without ever giving the students an opportunity to participate in the decision-making. While we might produce students who can read and write everything the teacher says, we haven't produced students who can think for themselves and who are active members of the community.

Mark: One of the things that come to mind is Glasser. He says we have to get rid of the "boss" mentality. We should invite students to be full members of the classroom. It is as much their classroom as it is the teacher's. The role change involves taking a new stance towards the profession.

Part of the school's mission is to produce lifelong learners. There's no reason for someone to feel like there's nothing much to do. If we help students while they're in school become lifelong learners with some kind of control over the things that they're learning, we really enrich their lives beyond whether they're successful today in the classroom; we make a dent in whether they're going to be successful in life.

Laurie: Teachers are lifelong learners, too. We need to allow the teachers to feel that their judgment is important and respected. They conference with students, work with students on an individual basis, and really know what's working, what's not working for the individual student. Too often schools fail to take advantage of teachers' abilities and knowledge; schools have "teacher-proofed" the process of education. Using portfolios puts respect back into the profession and allows respect for both students and teachers.

Rob: Portfolios can be characterized by words such as "collaborative," "cooperative," "partnership," "literacy-based." One of the key things about portfolios is the fact that it provides a vehicle by which students and teachers can be sure that there are links with the important literacy experiences the students have, in and out of school, as well as assessment links that are productive rather than judgemental. Portfolio assessment helps students link with other students and link with the teacher in a collaborative partnership.

Portfolios help us achieve a movement towards having assessment which is clearly grounded in the classroom, clearly grounded in recognizing that we should be helping the child develop as a decision-maker.

Portfolios begin to provide teachers with something akin to what a tax receipt organizer would provide a taxpayer in preparation for an audit. If, in fact, we're wanting accountability, it's important that we begin to help teachers and students organize themselves so that they don't become accountable to things which are alien but to things which are grounded in the reality of their own experiences.

Facilitating the Development of Meaningful Writing

Carolyn: One of the things that becomes apparent with portfolios is that students are doing a lot of different kinds of writing—journal writing, poetry, and so forth, which might be personal. Do you want to make comments on the kind of environment or the spirit of the classroom that would allow students to take that kind of risk to be able to produce materials that are meaningful to themselves?

Mark: There are a couple of issues with respect to the question. The first is that it goes along with the teacher's role. Over the last

10 years, teachers have become much more knowledgeable of reading and writing and how to get students involved in choosing their own reading and writing topics. I think that's great. It means a new focus on what we call generative work. We want students to be generating things that are their own stories. That might be an expository story or it might be a poem. The teacher needs to be accepting of the kinds of things students produce.

Second, time is a crucial element in the classroom, but students need time to produce meaningful pieces of work. Teachers need to provide time for students to work, time where they can think about and generate meaningful pieces, time to read and discuss books. Providing time for students to share their writing and their thoughts about books, providing time for students to work in collaboration with other students—those are the kinds of things that teachers can do I think that really facilitate the kind of environment where students can be generative.

Laurie: I think there's another important facet of the classroom environment which involves respect. This, again, is part of the teacher's role, and includes respect for everyone's writing, privacy, sharing, and for the idea that it takes time to work through a piece. First drafts aren't always wonderful and sometimes the last draft still becomes a work in progress. There is a developmental process that's going on with writing. Respecting the process and each other becomes a very important component of the portfolio classroom. It is important to recognize the student's ownership of the portfolio.

Time Management in the Portfolio Classroom

Carolyn: What kind of time commitment does it take for teachers to implement portfolios in the classrooms? How do teachers deal with time issues?

Mark: Over the years of working with lots of teachers using portfolios, especially teachers in transition from a text/basal-oriented classroom toward a literature-based reading-writing classroom, initially time is an important issue because they feel frustrated. In essence, they're trying to run two classrooms. Portfolios don't take any more time, but during the transition something has to give.

Managing portfolios involves a refocusing. Instead of doing a lot of group things or working out of a particular textbook or workbook, time can be allotted differently so that teachers are using that time to work with individuals, conferencing with individuals. Maybe working with some small groups. It's a question of setting priorities differently and of using the classroom time differently, more than it is taking more time.

Rob: I think you've got to define what takes time in portfolios. Developing the materials included in portfolios doesn't take time, since the portfolio is intended to represent things that are already going on in the classroom. Arranging to get students to pull together, reflect, review, share, and evaluate the portfolio will take the time.

What is key is to realize that what's taking time is instructionally worthwhile. As teachers have gotten involved in portfolios, many have had students at the end of a quarter pull together the showcase portfolio. This is not just a sort of clerical activity; it is an opportunity for the students to look back at what they have done over the quarter, what they have achieved, sometimes what they haven't achieved, what future goals they might have.

We're not talking about inordinate amounts of time. We're talking about things taking probably two or three days, thirty to forty minutes per day, to look over their work and discuss it with their classmates. There is also the opportunity oftentimes in classrooms for students to share their portfolios with others. We've found that teachers haven't really taken new time to do that. Typically, they have in place structures for students to share with a group. Instead of sharing a single piece, the teacher has students share their portfolios.

Where time becomes an issue is in terms of their conferencing with the students individually about their portfolios. My view with respect to that is that I would love teachers once a quarter to be able to conference with a student on his portfolio and to take 15 minutes out or 5 minutes out to do that with every student. That may be unrealistic. Perhaps a teacher could conference with the students "on the run" or in conjunction with parent nights.

Mark: But if the teachers have been conferencing with students all along on those pieces of writing, they have a pretty good idea of what's in their portfolios.

Rob: So maybe the teacher shouldn't view it as a conference with the student but as serving as a consultant.

Mark: It's refocusing. Looking at where that individual child is and how they can work with that child.

Rob: We've worked with probably 50 teachers at this point. I do not know a teacher who would say that it isn't worth the time that it takes.

Laurie: The things that are most important are the kinds of abilities we want the students to develop. We want students to have the opportunities to reflect on what they've done, to begin to be able to assess for themselves what's good about their work or what's not so good, to consider how they can improve, and to be able to make a decision that a piece finished to that point. When you start to value these abilities, the time also doesn't seem to be as much of a factor because you see instruction is still ongoing and valuable.

Each teacher has to develop routine ways of conferencing or talking to the students. Different teachers find different ways to feel comfortable. Some teachers take quick notes after they've talked to a student so that they have some sort of running record of what's going on with the student, or they develop other methods over time to help them feel like they're on top of what's in the portfolios.

Rob: At the very minimum I would think that portfolios would need to be done with a class of students once in a course of study. In elementary school that would be at least once a year. I'd like to see it done more and be an integral part of the classroom experience. Ideally, it should be woven into the fabric of the classroom.

Laurie: I don't think that once a year is enough. If the students haven't had experience assessing and talking about their strengths and weaknesses, you're not going to get a real in-depth analysis of their work. This isn't something that can just happen once and the student can be successful. It's something that needs to be an ongoing part of the curriculum.

Mark: The benefits for the students grow the more that they have to deal with their reflections. The more that they have to deal with what they've done, the better they become at assessing their work. Initially, students will start out at relatively mundane levels. They look at surface features of writing, and maybe they only see certain aspects of their pieces. They don't see them as a whole. The more that they're engaged in reflecting on their work, choosing their work, analyzing the work, the better that they become at doing those kinds of tasks. If we say that it's valuable for students to reflect on their work, to make decisions, to see where it is that they have to improve, then I think that we need to make provisions for that to happen often. It does have to be interwoven into the classroom.

Working With Parents and Administration

Planning for portfolio assessment involves negotiation as teachers tailor this tool to fit their goals, classrooms, and students.

Rob: With respect to time, teachers also need to think about working with the parents; that is, keeping the parents informed as to what's going on and how to interact with the students with respect to portfolios.

Teachers need to communicate clearly with the school administration as to what they're trying to do, what the rationale is, and so on. They need to think carefully about what the ramifications of portfolios might be in terms of report cards, grading, the possibility of dealing with state mandates, and the ways in which portfolios can be used to complement or substitute for state mandates, along with time spent actually in the classroom working with students.

Laurie: Teachers have to help parents and administrators feel comfortable that they know the skills and abilities and developmental levels of their students. In that way, even when they aren't using a basal series with everything spelled out, everyone feels comfortable that the students are progressing and that the teacher knows what is going on with the students.

Mark: What we're talking about is professionalism.

Laurie: The teachers know their craft.

Mark: That's right. Along with that comes a lot of responsibility because now we're saying that teachers have to know how to intervene with students, what's expected at certain developmental levels. They have to be, in some sense, diplomats because while you certainly want children to be working on things that are interesting to them, we all know you're going to have students that aren't quite sure what to be working on. Some students are going to need more help with making some of those decisions. That's okay, because that's part of the teacher's job.

We are saying that teachers are professionals, they can make those kind of decisions, and indeed they should make the decisions based on their day-to-day contacts with students.

Conferencing with Students

Rob: Part of the danger with portfolios is that people might lose sight of the goals that we've talked about and displace them with a formalization of the approach. Self-assessment is one such area. In some classrooms we're seeing teachers gravitate to having students conference about their portfolios in terms of a preset criteria for which the students have had little opportunity for input. It hasn't grown from the students. Our fear is that what we're seeing there is like the composition codes that were so prevalent in the classrooms, that weren't carefully tied to a specific writing event and didn't grow out of the individual as much as conferencing did.

Mark: To build on that, Lucy Calkins calls that the "front stoop" conference. Conferencing is an informal talk. Certainly the teacher knows what some of the qualities are and what the qualities that the piece might be lacking. There is that spirit in the conference where the child is leading the conference, but with an informed questioner. The teacher knows when and where to intervene and to make some suggestions. It's that subtle art of teaching; of helping the child feel valuable and at the same time making a comment about a particular thing so an aspect receives attention. Decisions are guided by the child's agenda, by being aware of the individual's needs, academic goals, and personal concerns.

Rob: Teachers have to develop the art of getting students to talk about compositions and for teachers to talk about compositions on their terms and not terms that come out of an English grammar book or English language arts books. If the criteria that teachers use to talk about students' compositions were part of a film review in the local newspaper, people would respond hysterically. We need to get students to begin to be able to talk about their work in the conferencing and in self-assessment. Just the way people talk about a film.

Mark: So many teachers that we've worked with say, after conferencing with students on portfolios, that they're shocked with how much they know about their students. They end up saying: "I don't need a textbook to tell me where to go with this student. I can see. It's right here in front of us where I need to go. I not only know what the child's needs are but I know about the child as a human being." One of the richest things that has come out of our work with teachers and portfolios is the knowledge that teachers have developed about their students and how good they feel about knowing their students intimately.

The Range of Children's Portfolios

Carolyn: What types of things can you expect to see in a child's portfolio?

Mark: The content of portfolios changes drastically as children move through school; from kindergarten through high school. We've seen certainly some very sophisticated portfolios from high school students who have done things on computer disks that are, to me, amazing. They're interactive; they're wonderful. They encompass a historical perspective of the child. There are very sophisticated portfolios that go across different content areas and include different forms of writing to kindergartners whose first attempts at writing are in portfolios, including labels for pictures, pictures from stories that the teacher has read, things the students value as kindergartners.

Teachers often help students use portfolios as a way to chronicle their growth into becoming users of reading and writing for certain tasks. In the middle grades we see students that include writing about books in their portfolios. They have pieces that share their thinking about their reading and how they feel about their reading, much more than just what the text was about but pieces that really begin analyzing that text from their own viewpoint. Where the real value comes is when we see students who begin to become experts at certain forms of writing and want to show that off. Whether it's a poet or a story writer, we have students who begin to find a niche for themselves.

The same is true with reading. There might be students that go through and chronicle their reading in series of books or of non-fiction books. The nice thing is that the portfolios reflect the wide interests and versatility that the students have.

Laurie: You can expect to see the students. With the portfolio that's what you truly discover. You learn where the students are, the things students care about, and those things which aren't as important to them; things they're good at and things they're not so good at. You can sit down and look at the portfolio and you know something about the student before you ever even meet the student.

Rob: Oftentimes students will bring things in from home. We had students who were bringing in the lyrics that went along with popular music, lyrics that they had written themselves, or letters that they had written. In a sense the portfolio became somewhat like a photo album or a scrap book, but one that had multidimensional proportions.

One concern teachers have as they look towards portfolios as assessment tools, including the possibility of making comparisons across groups of students, is to make sure that portfolios represent a range of different things, including students' best efforts over different genres in writing. The danger that you have with the students' portfolio is that you may not get the range unless you discuss it with the students ahead of time.

Sometimes teachers keep a section of the portfolio for things they prescribe. For example, in some classrooms teachers kept an audio tape of each child's oral reading. They were interested in seeing across time how these students fared in terms of their oral reading strategies. Other teachers require students to keep logs of their reading and writing.

Mark: You get the range by talking to the students in group sessions and by saying this can be a valuable component of their portfolios. You get a wide range by asking students to consider the benefits of developing versatility in their portfolios. Teachers can provide guidance through using examples, questioning, and discussing shared portfolios.

Portfolios and Grading

Rob: The student might have done what you consider, as a teacher, an incredible piece about a visit of an aunt and he decides to not include that but to include a piece on a super hero that's got a nifty sketch or something that he's really excited by. When we think about grading, we have to realize that what you may see in the portfolio may not represent the full range and the potential richness that you want. Sometimes the teachers will negotiate what goes in the portfolios with the students. Some teachers will actually add things to the student's portfolio or will have a supplemental portfolio which is part of their class file, as ways of making sure that the range is in there.

The use of portfolios doesn't necessarily preclude duplication of material. I would hate to see portfolios displacing the possibility of a student's work appearing in the classroom library. Or the possibility that a student's work might appear in an institutional portfolio as well as the student's portfolio. There are things I think teachers have to truly work out in schools and districts.

Mark: When I was using portfolios in my classroom, I developed a teacher's portfolio on the children, too. They had their portfolio that they were developing and certainly I had input into that, but at the same time there was other information that I felt like I needed on students: notes from conferences that we've had, my anecdotal records, spelling inventories that I did with students to get a better understanding of how I could help them develop as spellers, pieces that they didn't include in their portfolio but that I really liked and that I had asked them if I could include a copy of that in my collection of their work. For some students I included informal reading inventories that I did to get a better understanding of them as readers.

I needed this kind of thing to develop a teacher portfolio on students which broadened my view of students. We need multiple forms of assessment in classrooms. The students' portfolios are one form, but we also can't lose sight that teachers need a variety of information. I found it helpful to think of the other information that I collected as my teacher's portfolio on each student.

Rob: In terms of grading, ideally we wouldn't have teachers grading the student's portfolio, giving them A's and B's and C's. We would much more be interested in helping that child assess him or herself and doing some sort of collaborative report.

Mark: A reflective narrative.

Rob: That's right. Teachers need to develop the ability to do that. It's an area which is typically not covered in workshops, courses, or as part of staff development.

The same with report cards. In a whole language classroom I think it's a mistake to think that you should use a single report card form for every student. We've got to develop ways of approaching our students so that each student is viewed and treated uniquely.

Laurie: With grades, we get students to start thinking about their rank in the class, something is better and something is worse, or one of the students is good and I'm bad.

I heard two little girls the other day who were first graders. They were looking through picture books. One said to the other, "Here, this one has simpler words. You'll be able to read this." It wasn't a judgment and it wasn't taken that way. I thought it was great, because it just showed the students valuing each other where they were at that point and valuing the way they were developing. Not as this one is better than the other one. It's just this student is different from the other one.

Mark: The nice thing about portfolios is that they can literally fit into any grading scheme that is being currently used. If a school district uses A,B,C,D they can use the same kind of criteria to grade portfolios if they need to do that. At the same time what we've seen happen probably with all the teachers that we've worked with is, as they work with portfolios, they see the value in a more descriptive form of assessment.

Rob: A descriptive form which includes a wider variety of things entering into what might be graded or considered as part of the description.

Laurie: You never want to look at any one thing as an indicator of what a child knows or doesn't know. When you're talking about assessments, you want to look at a broad base of different measures over time, in different settings, and in different situations.

Mark: But there again it's that idea that teachers are empowered, and as teachers use portfolios, they have a sense of what's important for their particular grade level or class. What we've seen happening is that teachers are talking about changing the ways that they report. In report cards, in parent conferences. They are including portions of the portfolio in district cumulative records. Teachers are seeing the value of including a broader picture of the child.

Rob: As teachers do grade students with portfolios, the menu which they use for grading increases. Typically grades in the past have focused just on achievement. All of a sudden we're looking at where that child has come from, what his goals have been, what effort he has put in, and what improvement he has made across a range of things. Teachers who use portfolios move beyond a single achievement grade.

Laurie: It goes back to what you value. If you're looking at effort and involvement being important, then you're going to start valuing that in your assessment, too.

Rob: The portfolios do pick up the students who we sometimes call the "hoppers" because they hop from one thing to the next and don't really get much done. That's okay because sometimes they might get enough done to really reflect upon it and gain something. You've got to watch for that.

There is another side of evaluation which we've got to talk about. Teachers should also realize that they can use the contents of the portfolio, if they plan ahead, as substitutions for the state mandates. Instead of collecting another writing sample or collecting the students' responses to certain passages, they can find in their portfolios bench marks which would actually serve the purpose of state assessment. Teachers can say to the state: You want to know how this child writes? You want to see how this student has been reading? We've got this information for you.

Portfolios can be used as a replacement for and complement to state assessment. In one district, where a child was not going to be promoted based upon a standardized test result, they looked in the student's portfolio and saw what he had really done. They made the decision not to retain.

Mark: That's powerful. Teachers understand the value of what we're talking about. They also understand that in many cases parents may not initially understand some of the changes that are occurring. Part of this is parent education, informing parents about some of the changes that are occurring in the classroom; why some of those changes are occurring; what some of the values are that portfolios facilitate.

Every teacher that we've worked with has made some contact with parents in efforts to help them understand the changes that are occurring, and without fail the teachers have felt embraced by the parents. It's not that the parents demand grades. The teachers that we've worked with are substituting rich descriptions of what that "A" really means or "B" or "C" really means. They're talking about traits or characteristics of the students. Parents value that kind of information. Certainly teachers can still let the parents know if this is falling within grade level expectations. Parents want to have some kind of information, and if no other information is being given to them, then they are going to want grades. The teachers that have taken some initiative to contact parents and to work with them have been embraced by parents.

Portfolios and Self-evaluation

Carolyn: What sort of self-evaluation can you expect with students?

Mark: Interestingly, students like to evaluate their own writing. They like to write about what it is they think are strengths. They might focus on surface structures. Their evaluations grow during the course of the year.

Students don't evaluate pieces based on adult standards. It's really very refreshing because they see things from a more personalized perspective. They make comments on a piece because it was a particularly meaningful event. That's why they want to remember it and that's why they have included it in their portfolio. But that shows that they're valuing the writing process and the purpose of writing.

One of the things that happens, though, with teachers facilitating self-evaluation and sharing those self-evaluations over the course of the year, students' self-evaluations expand so that they do cover adult expectations, personal expectations, affective. They reveal their feelings, but it takes a long time.

Traditionally we've looked at school as being chopped up into little bits and pieces. We do this for forty minutes. We move onto this for forty minutes and we move onto this for forty minutes. The view that portfolios precipitate is that the school year is seen as an entity. We want students to grow during the course of that year. Given time to do that, their personal evaluations become much richer. They are able to evaluate mechanical things about their pieces as well as things about content, organization, and style. But it takes time to develop that kind of eye.

Laurie: In literature-based, whole language classrooms, reading and writing are seen as something that's integral, something that works together. Students see a lot of evaluation happening all the time. You read a book and the students think it's neat and you talk about why it is neat. They start thinking about how the author wrote and to decide how it applies to their own writing. They learn to see themselves as they see published authors and to value the craft of writing. They have learned that their contemporaries, their peers also do neat things when they write or the teacher does neat things when he or she writes. It becomes part of the atmosphere of the classroom. What they're doing is not so unique because it's what is happening around them all the time. That takes time, but it is a whole atmosphere that develops. Portfolios can help to foster that kind of atmosphere.

The Spectrum of Portfolio Proposals

Rob: What do we see as the spectrum? How do we see our ideas fitting in with portfolio proposals that are being pushed forward?

Mark: A lot of people are now moving toward authentic kinds of assignments like portfolios. There are several problems in portfolios that I've seen to this point. One is that initially teachers want to have control over the portfolio, which means that portfolios become another assignment and students aren't necessarily involved in the critical part of the decision making—what goes in the portfolio, comparing and contrasting their pieces and making important decisions about their own achievements and goals—which, I think, is probably at the heart of it.

Laurie: As teachers begin to develop their understanding of portfolios, the portfolios themselves range from a folder that just contains an accumulation of a student's work for the year to something that is a much more active and process-oriented and which allows students to compare and contrast their effort as well as their process of achievement.

Mark: For teachers who are making a transition to a more literature-based classroom, it's difficult to give up the control. And I think that part of the problem, too, is if you're looking for just skills in student writing instead of helping students understand themselves as writers—which means seeing the writing in a whole form—then it's much easier to use them as another teacher tool instead of allowing students to have control.

Laurie: Portfolios became more student-centered, which is an advantage. They go beyond just the reading and writing and incorporate how students think about themselves as students and individuals.

Rob: Our proposal is driven by a desire to get the students actively involved, a desire to allow the portfolio to represent the literacy artifacts which actually grow out of the classroom, their lives outside of school, rather than being imposed on them. I would characterize our proposal as child centered versus institutionalized. Although there may be some requirements pertaining to portfolios emanating from the state or school district, they wouldn't dominate or subvert it from being student owned.

Mark: Yes. The teacher in a collaborative classroom is part of the group. If the teacher has recommendations or suggestions or even certain criteria that they would like to see in the portfolio, they can certainly bring that out in the group format with the class and discuss those criteria along with all kinds of suggestions that students have for portfolios. There are times, especially if teachers are going to want to use portfolios for accountability to school districts or to the state, there may be certain things that they need to make sure are in the portfolio. But I don't think that those kind of things should take away from the child's ownership.

Final Words on Portfolios

We want to close with five thoughts about portfolios in class-rooms:

1. This book is not the definitive account of portfolios. We encourage you to read our ideas thoughtfully and critically and to reflect upon them and to implement them in your own way.

2. We would encourage people to be thoughtful and careful as they read other people's presentations of portfolios. We are hesitant about some of the discussions of portfolios, particu-larly those that are solely intent on the institutionalization of portfolios; that is, those where the district is going to mandate what the portfolio will be and what it will include.

3. Related to where we think portfolios are—our work has been a research and development effort—if we were to write this book in a year's time we would write something different. This book has taken three years to write and over that three years it has been revised and revised—not just at the level of surface text but substantially in terms of the ideas. The areas that we're wrestling with right now are in the area of getting students involved in self-assessment and the whole issue of how do we use portfolios also to meet the demands of the institutional accountability.

4. We would hope that just as we are approaching these thing with a research and development orientation, that teachers do so as well. We hope teachers think about these issues, try them out, and experiment with them by watching students and finding out how other people are exploring these issues.

5. Finally, we fear the teacher who takes the ideas in this book and sees them as a formula. We're interested in improving as-sessment in classrooms so it empowers teachers, students, and parents. We hope teachers develop that spirit of owner-ship and empowerment in their classroom efforts and ap-proach their efforts with a research and development attitude.

══════Chapter 2══════

Toward a Theory of Assessment

This book is intended to help you orient your assessment practices so that assessment has a working relationship with teaching and learning. We believe that assessment should empower teachers, students, and parents; that worthwhile classroom practices should be ignited and not extinguished by assessment; and that students should view assessment as an opportunity to reflect upon and celebrate their effort, progress, and improvement, as well as their processes and products.

It may appear that we are asserting that portfolios are a powerful assessment tool. This is only partially true. It is you, the classroom teacher, and your students who are the most important assessment tools in the classroom. We believe that the teachers and the students, rather than tests devised by others, should be the crucial element in assessing growth and progress in the classroom.

Before we begin to discuss the use of portfolios it is important to reflect on what we mean by assessment. What do we see as the current state of assessment in schools? What are the underlying principles that should guide assessment? What role should teachers assume? What is the relationship of students to assessment? How should parents be involved?

The State of Testing in Schools

There are major problems with assessment in schools. In

particular, we are concerned that:

1. Testing appears to consume enormous amounts of instructional time that seems difficult to justify given the nature of the tests and purposes for which they are used.
2. The reasons for administering tests represent a restricted array of purposes, and many of these purposes may be difficult to justify if examined in terms of the goals associated with a child-centered view of literacy development.
3. Most tests do not mirror the nature of literacy that is occurring in today's classrooms.
4. Most tests appear to reflect assumptions that either run counter to current views of reading and writing or, at best, reflect a rather restricted view.
5. The stature of formal tests tend to disenfranchise teachers and constrain, rather than enhance, teaching practices.
6. Students are viewed as the subjects of testing rather than partners or clients in the testing enterprise. Student self-assessment has long been ignored in the classroom.

Before addressing these concerns in more detail, let us explain the basis for our concerns by addressing the data that deal with:

1. The amount of testing occurring in schools;
2. The purposes of tests;
3. The nature of tests.

Amount of Testing in Schools

It seems that an enormous amount of testing occurs in schools when the various types of testing to which students are exposed is added to the time devoted to preparing for such tests. Currently test sales are at an all-time high as test publishers and publishers of reading programs offer spurious promises of educational improvement by accountability. Rough estimates suggest that a large percentage of children in this country receive more than 2,000 test items every year — including items on standardized tests, basal tests, and teacher-made tests. Furthermore, surveys of teachers suggest that on average fourteen hours are spent over the course of a year preparing students for standardized tests (six hours preparing for commercial tests, six hours for state tests, two hours for district tests), twenty-six for basal tests, eighteen hours for teacher-made tests.

Why be bothered with the amount of testing? We are bothered for several reasons. First, we do not think tests contribute to student learning. In our informal surveys with test takers, we have found that most tests engender anxiety and fear rather than fulfillment. Ask yourself: Did testing enhance your learning? Did testing engender anxiety? Second, testing is taking time away from learning when time is a precious commodity in schools. In almost every conversation we have had recently with teachers and students about teaching and learning, time is identified as one of the key factors that interferes with what teachers and students want to be able to achieve.

Who Controls Testing?

Are teachers the victims or the perpetrators of testing? Are administrators, state department personnel or politicians responsible? Do students have a voice? The answer to the first two questions seems yes and no. The answer to the third is no.

While teachers might act as if they have little say over what is assessed, a recent survey of the testing practices of elementary and secondary teachers in the United States (Valencia & Pearson, in press) suggests that teachers do an enormous amount of testing during the school year, and a large proportion of it falls under their auspices. In particular, while teachers might be required to administer standardized tests once or twice a year, a great deal of other testing occurs in their classrooms that they control in various ways. For example, the survey reports the following: 91 percent of teachers give basal tests three or more times every year; 22 percent report giving basal tests nine or more times a year; 64 percent give teacher-made tests three or more time a year; 37 percent report that they give teacher-made tests nine or more times a year.

Increasingly, when principals are asked to indicate how frequently teacher-made tests are administered the percentages are slightly higher—namely, principals perceive that 78 percent of the teachers create and administer their own tests three or more times per year; 48 percent feel teachers do so nine or more times per year.

Apart from teacher-made tests, some 92 percent of teachers report using observations of students to assess their students; 70 percent report using structured observation forms; and 90 percent of teachers report using assignments.

The problem arises that the tests that the teachers administer might not count as much as those legislated by politicians, mandated by state departments, and focused on by administrators and teachers.

The Purpose of Testing

Why are we testing so much? There appears to be a host of

possible reasons for testing in schools. They include:
- Making policy decisions;
- Evaluating a program's effectiveness;
- Assessing whether or not students are achieving certain standards;
- Informing curricular decisions;
- Rewarding or penalizing certain groups;
- Giving students feedback;
- Having an opportunity to collaborate with students.

State departments and legislators often cite determining and assuring standards, allocating resources, and ensuring ongoing improvement as reasons for testing. Regardless of whether or not tests can be used for any of these purposes, they tend to pursue the first two goals rather than the last one. Teachers are more likely to say that tests are used to plan curricula and to grade students than to say that they are used to involve students as collaborators in such efforts.

What Do Reading and Writing Tests Measure?

To address the question, a quick reminder of what most reading and writing tests look like may be worthwhile. Most form reading tests involve the use of a multiple choice format with a single right answer in conjunction with passages that tend toward being a special kind of genre just for tests— namely, snippets of fiction and nonfiction. Even at the kindergarten levels, multiple choice formats prevail. Typical of the types of items and passages that are included in these tests are the illustration (right).

Students' responses are then usually added for purposes of comparison with other students to determine a grade.

Fill in the circle for the word that has the same or almost the same meaning as the word in dark type.

1. **afraid**
   - ○ strong
   - ● scared
   - ○ happy

2. **entire**
   - ○ whole
   - ○ part
   - ● piece

3. **begin**
   - ○ finish
   - ● start
   - ○ keep

4. **silly**
   - ○ tiny
   - ○ funny
   - ○ sad

Fill in the circle to answer the questions about the story.

Tailor Bird

One of the most interesting birds I have seen is the Indian Tailor Bird. They are small olive green birds that don't look at all unusual, but they have a most unusual way of making their nests. The birds work together in pairs. First they find a leaf, the right size, and make holes along the edges with their beaks. Through these holes they thread grass. One bird pushes the thread from the outside, while the other bird sits in the nest and pushes it back until the edges of the leaf are sewn together to make a kind of bag, still hanging on the tree, in which the Tailor Bird lays its eggs.

What do Tailor Birds use as thread?
- ○ Grass
- ○ String
- ○ Spider web
- ○ Thorns

The Tailor Birds are interesting because they
- ○ are small and olive green in color.
- ○ live in pairs.
- ○ make their nests in a special way.
- ○ fly very fast.

The Tailor Bird got that name because it
- ○ is a small bird.
- ○ looks unusual.
- ○ can sew.
- ○ has a beak shaped like a needle.

Ease of administration, ease of scoring, and ease of trans-
forming a student score into a grade seem to be the overriding
motivation for the test structure and practice. Unfortunately,
these benefits appear to override the fact that a reader's responses to a set of multiple choice items might not be a fair
sample of reading abilities because:

- A predetermined response is the only acceptable answer
  for each question;
- A student's understanding is either "right" or "wrong"
  rather than partial or different;
- A specific set of passages or paragraphs will not adequately sample the reading abilities of a student;
- The measure of the student's reading ability is the extent
  to which the student can read snippets and choose from
  somebody else's set of possible responses their choice of
  the preferred response;
- A score or grade based upon the total of correct choices
  reflects the student's reading ability.

The typical writing assignment requires students to write an
essay for a specified topic that is then scored against agreed upon
standards. The Educational Testing Service and a number of
school districts have rubrics or scoring guides that involve
standards for content, style, form, and mechanics to which
examiners are expected to agree as they assess student writing.
On the positive side, the assessment of writing is not plagued
with the widespread use of multiple choice items, though such
writing assessments exist. Furthermore, writing assessment affords students the opportunity to develop their own ideas. On the
negative side, they do so typically in response to somebody else's
(other than the writer's) assignment. Essentially they measure
the writer's forced response in accordance with somebody else's
standards.

Missing from both the assessment of reading and writing are:
- The use of reading and writing together;
- An open-ended understanding of why students read and
  write;
- Judging readers' and writers' responses on their terms;
- An interest in the differences that emerge across a range of
  "authentic" situations involving reading and writing;
- An appreciation of effort and process;
- An interest in discovery and idiosyncratic learning rather
  than in judging students in terms of standards that reflect
  conventionality.

In essence, most formal assessment devices represent a
genre unto themselves. What is measured on these tests fails to
approach what we view as literacy and the changes that are

occurring in classrooms. As a result, one must ask oneself if most scores derived from these tests misrepresent the nature of reading abilities and, therefore, have little predictive utility.

Problems with Testing

With these considerations as a foundation, we believe that the following problems exist with testing.

PROBLEM 1:

Tests reflect an outdated view of classrooms and restricted goals for learning.

In Duluth, Minnesota, two fifth grade students asked their teacher, "Why are we doing all of this discussion and writing if this is not what is on the tests?"

In Columbus, Ohio, the first question asked by students was, "How will this be graded?" When they realized that grades were based upon how a project looked and a test of the facts, they played it safe and focused upon what their projects looked like and attended to the facts likely to be tested. Meanwhile, the teacher was frustrated with their lack of investment and motivation for doing the projects. Not surprisingly when students were asked to share their projects, they did not ask questions or discuss interesting issues. Instead, students did little more than politely listen to each other's presentations as they jotted down testable facts.

Standardized and formal classroom testing are removed from the teaching and learning that naturally occurs in the classroom. Portfolios shift classroom assessment from formal to informal, from anxiety-producing to supportive, from uni-dimensional to multi-dimensional, and from isolated to collaborative.

Both teachers and students paint a bleak picture about the current uses of formal tests in their classrooms and how they relate to their goals. Teachers attribute to formal tests a rather narrow view of what tests measure. The following are comments by teachers about testing.

- The items on the tests do not reflect what we teach in our classrooms.
- The test items are not representative of the kinds of work that students do daily.
- Tests do not reveal what kids really do.

Students' comments suggest similar concerns:

- Tests and how we are graded do not reward experimentation or getting into new ideas.
- They want to be sure we got it their way. They are not so interested in me.

The mismatch between what is taught and what is measured should come as no surprise. Oftentimes, ease of administration takes precedence over including the kinds of open-ended activities that may exist in classrooms. Also, tests may reflect a view of reading and writing that is quite dated and, as a result, less valid. Lee Cronbach (1971), one of the foremost test and measurement scholars of this century, argues that tests developed in one decade are apt to be inappropriate in another. Unfortunately, testing practices in reading and writing have changed very little for almost thirty years. Table 1 (see page 29) outlines the contrast between current practices in teaching reading and writing and the testing practices used to assess the learning of reading and writing skills.

In past years, reading programs required students to respond to segments of texts artificially constrained by vocabulary controls. Nowadays, with the advent of reading/writing and literature-based curricula, reading and writing are less frequently taught in separate, neatly packaged units than the traditional tests reflect. In classroom situations where reading, writing, and other language arts are integrated, reading and writing occur simultaneously. Teachers are interested in how writers use reading as a springboard and how readers use writing to reflect upon and to develop meanings. There is a host of other developments that have occurred or are occurring, including:

- Tradebooks are replacing graded readers;
- Collaboration and cooperative learning are replacing individual worksheet activities;
- Response and discussion are replacing teachers questions;
- Journals and extended responses are replacing workbook pages;
- Projects and units in which stories and writing activities are tied together are replacing the reading of single selections and one-time writing assignments;
- Reading and writing skills are presented less lock-step in a rigid sequence with mastery;
- Individual selection of reading materials and writing activities have replaced teacher assigned topics and selections.

PROBLEM 2:

Formal tests reflect a limited view of reading and writing.

In many ways, traditional reading and writing tests do not live up to the standards that come from an expanded and evolving view of literacy. An expanded view of literacy would include an interest in assessing:

- What learners read and write;
- How learners read and write;
- Why learners read and write;
- Their approach to reading and writing and their emerging goals and attitudes;
- The understandings and discoveries learners achieve as they read and write;
- The uses of these new learnings;
- The extent to which reading and writing empower student thinking;

Table 1

Practice	Current Testing Procedures
Reading and writing are taught together. Readers write in response to what they have read; writers read in conjunction with their writing.	Reading and writing are tested separately. Reading tests rarely include items requiring responses that involve extended writing; writing tests do not require students to read in conjunction with their writing.
Reading and writing programs often have the students select their own texts or topics, establish their own purposes, ask their own questions, develop their own meanings of text, share and compare own interpretations of texts with others, revise their interpretations.	Reading tests require the student to read a text selected by somebody without regard to interests and assess the student's understandings based upon his/her responses to somebody else's questions. Writing tests often do not include having the students write. If writing is involved, students are given the topic and purpose and are expected to work by themselves.
Reading programs are including more and more opportunities for students to read trade books that are not controlled for vocabulary or excerpted. Character development and story lines are usually in place.	Reading tests have students responding to very short paragraphs that are often lacking in character development or story line.
Reading and writing programs involve having students pull ideas together from multiple sources (several books, peer input, films, etc.).	Reading and writing tests are tied to a single text.
Reading and writing programs expect students to respond differently to different texts read and written for different purposes.	Reading and writing tests assume students' reading and writing performance is generally the same across all texts.
Reading and writing programs have as a goal the empowerment of students and the development of their independence. They have as goals the enjoyment of reading and the ability to self-initiate and self-assess.	Reading and writing tests do not address enjoyment, empowerment, self-initiation, and self-assessment.

Formal tests focus upon a narrow band of acquired under-standings—namely, whether students can produce according to established expectations.

Furthermore, formal tests seem largely to ignore some key findings from research on reading and writing. Whereas the research on reading comprehension and writing emphasizes the extent to which readers' or writers' background of experience and purpose will have an overriding impact on their understanding, tests tend to focus upon verbatim recall and judge reading comprehension by a predetermined standard of response. It is as if formal testing may be forcing readers and writers to hold in abeyance their own understanding. It is not surprising that in a number of studies researchers have found marked differences in how readers and writers approach tests and how they approach other reading and writing experiences. It is as if tests require learning the art of test taking and a set of behaviors that may be counterproductive in more authentic reading situations.

There are a number of other problems with tests. Tests assume that reading abilities can easily be summarized or totalled. The use of a single score or a total score that is then translated into a grade equivalent, stanine, or percentile rank ignores natural variation that is known to exist—namely, under-standings will and should vary across selections, situations, and across time. Assessment of writing also tends to disregard growth over time, range of writing pursued, use of resources, problem solving, reflection, and purposes achieved.

Formal testing, by its nature, has treated the complex task of assessment of reading and writing abilities as if it were simpler than it really is, and, in so doing, it has artificially neatened the process of language arts assessment. Such neatening has re-sulted in the misrepresentation of children's abilities to read and write.

We are not alone in arguing that such a mismatch exists. In a number of articles and papers (Johnston, 1984; Pearson & Valencia, 1987; Jett-Simpson, et al., 1990) similar concerns have been expressed. The following seven items outline some of these problems associated with the differences between reading and writing in the classroom, concerns that should be addressed by assessment, and current testing practices (adapted from Tierney and McGinley, 1990):

1. Readers and writers come from diverse backgrounds. Each person has a different purpose for reading and different understandings and interpretations, which results in dif-ferences in appropriate questions, summaries, and recalls. Writers' diverse backgrounds cause considerable variation in compositions from one situation to the next. Reading and writing assessment, then, must be able to account for divergent responses, which means it cannot be measured

by the fixed or absolute standards currently being used.

2. Should we assess students using fixed standards? Typically tests use multiple choice items for which there is an assumed correct answer. Is this viable? We would argue that each person's unique purpose, background, perspective, and sense of audience or authorship have pervasive and dynamic influences upon what he or she reads and writes. Reading and writing performance, therefore, should take into consideration the ways in which these factors interface with one another throughout the activities of reading and writing. Unfortunately, few assessments consider the interplay of reading and writing. Recent attempts to assess the impact of background knowledge, purpose, and selected behaviors fail to address their interplay or misconstrue them as static with single scores.

3. Can we assume that a single score can summarize a student's performance in reading or writing? In most test situations, student performance is summed across sets of test items. We question the viability of these practices. Reading and writing performances are not stable, nor can they be viewed as a unity; students respond differently to different tasks at different times in different settings. Measuring reading and writing by aggregating performance across texts, tasks, and settings misrepresents differential performances. Tests, however, tend to aggregate rather than differentiate performance. When there is differentiation of data in standardized tests, the groupings tend to be simplistic and do not adequately represent the complex interrelationship between an individual's reading and writing.

4. When tests are developed, is it reasonable to exclude those items that most students get right, or most get wrong, or items for which only certain students get right? No. Items should not be dropped based upon whether or not certain students respond to them correctly or incorrectly. Each item should be judged in terms of whether or not it is a question worth asking. Many tests are constructed to eliminate items that do not differentiate between "good" and "poor" readers or writers. Dropping "erratic" items contributes to a limited representation of student performance. Given the normal instability of reading and writing skills over time and tasks, these erratic test items should not be regarded as exceptional or anomolous.

5. Should we assess reading and writing only through paper and pencil tasks? We would argue that adequate assessment extends beyond that which can be represented on paper. The quality of thinking engaged during reading and writing may not appear on paper, in part, because it is

difficult for students to articulate. Various direct and indirect measures are needed if we are to capture the quality of thinking engaged during reading and writing.

6. Can we assume that the material included on tests is representative of what students should be reading and writing? To assess real-world reading and writing, students should be assessed in contexts that mirror or simulate such uses. Real-world tasks or simulations are rarely included in assessment batteries. Reading and writing are separated, and in both reading and writing tests the passages and tasks presented are distortions of real-world situations.

7. Should students be involved in assessment? A reader's or writer's perspective of his or her achievements and meaning-making skills is at the heart of assessment and empowering students to be effective decisionmakers. Assessment should be directed at helping students engage in self-assessment and evaluation of their own abilities. Self-assessment, unfortunately, is omitted from most assessment batteries, or it is assessed superficially (i.e., through selected items using rating scales).

PROBLEM 3:

Tests disenfranchise teachers and constrain instructional possibilities.

What appears to be a key consideration of the role of assessment is a tension between individual empowerment and governmental accountability. In most situations, the scales seem weighed heavily on the side of the governmental (national, state, and district level) to the detriment—perhaps disenfranchisement—of teacher and student. Rather than recognizing the importance of having faith in the teacher's ability to negotiate instruction based upon the unique needs of individual students, there seems to be an attempt by states, districts, and, now, the federal government to police performance through standards. The federal government, many states, and numerous districts seem intent on arranging a marriage between teaching and testing with little regard for the shortcomings of formal testing programs, as well as a lack of concern for empowering teachers and students as effective decisionmakers.

The costs are immense. The end result may be a mismatch between what is assessed and what should be assessed, who should be assessing and who is assessing, and what teachers and students should be pursuing and what they actually do.

Many school districts put aside time just to prepare students for these tests; likewise, publishers include example activities to ensure students involved in their programs have practiced certain types of test items. Moreover, such tests relegate the teacher to the role of a technician rather than an expert. The point is that testing places teachers and students in a role that is reactive rather than proactive. It is as if teachers and students have become clerks in their own classrooms, helpless to do anything other than to perpetuate the system they have internalized. Indeed, when given the chance, some teachers may opt to choose someone else's test rather than to use their own powers of observation, and students may express preferences for tasks in which they don't have to think.

PROBLEM 4:

Students are not engaged in self-assessment.

Do students seem empowered by tests? Our observations of students suggest that students find most tests to be anxiety producing, view tests as relatively non-informative, and question what they measure. In our analyses of students' views of tests and their assessment of themselves, we found that most students have a restricted view of their strengths and weaknesses, goals, and achievements, and they predominantly tend to have a negative view of themselves. It came as no surprise to read recently about the statement students in Torrance, California, purportedly wanted to make:

Students Subvert Own Scores
Torrance, Calif., May 2 (AP)

Seniors at a top-performing high school in this Los Angeles suburb sabotaged their answers on a recent annual test that measures schools' academic quality.

One of the students says the diminished scores were a rebellion against pressure to perform. But administrators at the school, West High, deny that there was too much pressure, and a spokeswoman for the State Department of Education suggests that the effort to drag down the school's score on the examination, the California Assessment Test, may have resulted from something else.

The results of the California Assessment Test are used to determine a school's academic placement among other schools in the state. The results are published in newspapers and are considered by the state for achievement awards and grants. In addition, prospective home buyers use the results when a good school district is a consideration.

West High School's reading scores in the test dropped from the 85th percentile statewide last year to the 51st percentile this year, and mathematics scores fell from the 95th percentile to the 71st percentile.

William Bawden, the school's principal, said a check of students' test booklets, which are not signed, had shown an unusual number of wrong answers in 18 booklets, including some booklets that contained no right answers. He said one student had admitted deliberately doing poorly.

The student body president, Kelle Price, said some seniors became disgruntled when teachers interrupted classes to prepare students for the test and when administrators visited classes to stress the importance of doing well on it.

New York Times, Education, May 3, 1989, p. 21.

The point is, shouldn't assessment empower learning and teaching rather than be detached from it? The current state of affairs in schools is that students are denied any substantive role in assessment. Their views of their progress or what they are trying to achieve along with their self-assessment is overlooked. Testing is not a partnership between student and teacher, self-assessment is not a goal, and as a result, assessment seems to remain detached from learning.

Ideally, we envision a classroom where students are involved in judging themselves with the support of teachers, peers, and parents. Self-assessment helps students to take steps toward becoming lifelong learners and assists students with taking responsibility for their learning processes and the work they produce. This kind of assessment requires a new kind of partnership between teacher and students—a partnership where teachers help students assess themselves. It requires viewing assessment as a goal for learning rather than an outcome.

Goals for Classroom-based Assessment

We believe that we need to move beyond current testing practices and to do so educators need to consider the desired outcome from the assessment procedures utilized. In other words, how might assessment become useful to teachers and students, better inform teachers and students about achievement, progress, and effort, and fuel teacher and student instructional collaborations?

As we take an appraisal of assessment it is important to be clear about what we need from our assessment efforts.

1. It is important for teachers to take a lead in being able to report to parents, district administrators, board members, and state departments valid information about how students are achieving and performing over time. Assessment

in today's society should provide accountability to involved and interested stakeholders.

2. Assessment should provide the information that is needed to pursue ongoing curriculum development that is responsive to student needs and therefore, provides directions for instructional decision making.

3. Assessment should consider definitions of literacy, including the range of different kinds of reading and writing experiences, as well as their facets. Rather than limiting assessment in reading and writing to a restricted set of subskills or outcomes, our view of what is measured and how it is measured should broaden assessment possibilities.

4. Assessment practices should involve the students. If we want students to develop into independent thinkers and successful performers they must have the skills, knowledge, and confidence to evaluate their own processes and products.

5. Through an effective assessment program teachers should grow in their knowledge about how children develop as readers and writers. Through this understanding, teachers can also continually evaluate their own performance. Teachers can ask themselves questions that reveal if what they are doing instructionally is truly making a difference in their student's growth in reading and writing.

6. Procedures for summarizing and reporting student performance should be consistent with what we purport to be measuring and developing. Current methods of practices for reporting literacy achievement are oftentimes scores or grades that do not translate into practice.

Assessment should provide all interested parties with information that illuminates the student growth that occurs as a result of collaborative contacts with teachers. It should also facilitate learning, appropriate instruction and students' awareness of their own strengths and needs as readers and writers and enhance teacher and curriculum development.

Features of a Classroom-based Assessment Program

The following characteristics summarize what we believe to be essential features of a classroom based assessment program that respects readers and writers in the process of learning and that meet the goals we have for assessment.

1. Assessment is based on what the child actually does. Student work and process are observed and analyzed to provide a rich view of progress, achievement, effort, strategies, and versatility.

2. Assessment addresses the reading and writing experiences

in which students are engaged.

3. Classroom assessment procedures should describe clearly and accurately how students do on a variety of tasks over an extended period of time. Decisions about students' strengths and needs are derived as a result of analyzing multiple samples of student work that have been collected during the course of the year and show the students' versatility.

4. Effective classroom assessment programs are designed to include the students as active participant in forming the reading and writing tasks, in developing assessment criteria, and in assessing their own effort, progress, achievement, attitude, and goal attainment.

5. An assessment program should be multifaceted. There should be provisions to assess more than just the final products. Assessment should focus on achievement, process, and quality of self-assessment.

6. Assessment is continuous and inseparable from instruction. It is an interactive and collaborative process in which information is collected in natural classroom instructional encounters (individual, small group, and whole group). Assessment should have a reciprocal relationship with the nature and goals of schools. That is, assessment should be informed by the nature and goals of schools and, in turn, inform these goals.

7. A yearly assessment plan guides the timing and use of a variety of assessment procedures. These procedures should work together to form a composite. It is likely that there are regular assessments that occur weekly, quarterly, and yearly. These assessments may be varied and serve slightly different purposes.

8. Assessment strengthens teacher's and student's knowledge. Assessment should contribute to a teacher's and student's understanding of themselves and each other. Teachers and students should find assessment empowering rather than beleaguering. Teachers and students should grow in their ability to make insightful analysis of the data gathered.

9. Record keeping and collections of work samples by both teachers and students provide the systematic information that facilitates communication.

10. The teacher is an expert evaluator, recognized and supported:
    - The teacher not only knows the nature of the learner's reading and writing but provides first-hand evidence of progress and achievement.
    - The teacher recognizes patterns by relating what

readers and writers are doing and thinking to knowledge of the learner and understanding of literacy.

- The teacher has the opportunity to observe the learner first-hand across a variety of situations including those in which learners are interested, have varying degrees of background knowledge, interact with others, or proceed independently.
- The teacher can explore the environments and situations that enhance learning.
- The teacher assesses what students have achieved in terms of effort, improvement, and process.
- The teacher assesses the learner's literacy development in the context of what learners are doing.
- The teacher pursues collaborative assessment with the learner, as well as the learner's ongoing assessment and development of self-assessment strategies.

11. The students' ability to assess themselves is viewed as a measure of how testing and assessment have a meaningful, ongoing, and working relationship with teaching.

12. Parental and other stakeholders' involvement in the assessment program is vital to supporting the learner's ongoing literacy development and the legitimization of assessment practices consistent with what literacy is and literacy instruction should be.

The subsequent chapters in this book describe how reading and writing portfolios fit into and facilitate a sound assessment program. We believe portfolios are a means of providing the depth and breadth of information to help teachers to put into practice a sound theory of assessment in their classrooms.

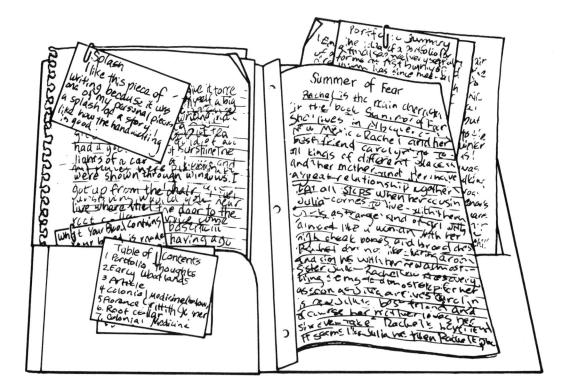

Chapter 3

An Introduction to Portfolios

Some Essentials of Portfolios

- Portfolios are systematic collections by both students and teachers. They can serve as the basis to examine effort, improvement, processes, and achievement as well as to meet the accountability demands usually achieved by more formal testing procedures. Through reflection on systematic collections of student work, teachers and students can work together to illuminate students' strengths, needs, and progress.
- Portfolios are not objects. They are vehicles for ongoing assessment by students. They represent activities and processes (selecting, comparing, self-evaluation, sharing, goal setting) more than they do products.
- Some of the values that underlie the use of portfolios include a belief in developing procedures for planning classroom learning that represents what students are actively doing; a commitment to student involvement in self-evaluation and helping students to become aware of their own development as readers and writers; a belief in the view that assessment should take into consideration: 1) the processes readers and writers enlist; 2) the products they develop; 3) the improvements they achieve; 4) the effort they put forth, as well as 5) how these features vary across a range of reading and writing.

Portfolios offer a new framework for assessment—one that facilitates student reflection in conjunction with reading and writing—a framework that responds to demands for student empowerment, the changing nature of classrooms, and a new consensus regarding the need for revamping testing practices. Portfolios offer a framework that is dynamic and grounded in what students are actually doing. It is a framework with the potential to empower both teachers and students to reflect upon their reading and writing and to grow in their understanding of their reading and writing, as well as themselves.

Portfolios engage students in an assessment and evaluation cycle. Working by themselves and with others, students will mull over their work, reflect on their efforts, and become actively involved in self-evaluation.

We hope teachers will develop portfolio practices that reflect the literacy experiences and character of their unique classrooms. We recognize the need for teachers to establish elements to be included in each student's portfolio; indeed, if portfolios are to replace formal testing practices, having some benchmarks in common may be essential. The problem, the fear, is with becoming overly prescriptive. One of a portfolio's key benefits is that it is a robust concept that allows for diversity. If standard guidelines are imposed, diversity may be displaced and student investment and self-assessment may become a secondary rather than primary concern. Therefore, we hope teachers will encourage students to customize their own portfolios and that the portfolio practice in each classroom will reflect a great number of possibilities for students to express their individual personalities, desires, and work styles.

The Origins of Portfolios in Other Fields

Portfolios are not as novel to other fields of endeavor as they are to reading and writing classrooms. Commercial artists, models, photographers, artists, and people in other fields of endeavor use portfolios to showcase their achievements and skills. Whether it is in conjunction with a journalist's resume—including examples of projects, by-line files, and stories—or an artist's collection of work, the portfolio is tangible evidence of accomplishments and skills that must be updated as a person changes and grows. For example, Mark, a journalism student at the Ohio State University, maintains two portfolios—a copy-editing portfolio and a news report portfolio. Mark uses them to reflect upon his work, to consider what he has achieved, and to put together samples of his work for job interviews. Since a journalist must revise, edit, and write headlines, cut lines, and catch lines. Mark's portfolios include a range of samples of his efforts.

Journalists keep portfolios which may include samples of their reporting, copy-editing, and/or layout.

Artists' portfolios vary considerably, and may include originals or photographs of work in several media.

Amy, a young artist, maintains a portfolio of her artwork. As Amy says, "these are pieces I feel happy with, that I have gotten feedback from, and that I feel content with, and that I'd like to show people." Although each piece included is not entirely finished, they are "finished to a point you feel that it's as far as you want to go with it. Some might be in process, at a sketch stage, so it may not be polished but it feels finished." When Amy wishes to represent her artwork to her friends, teachers, or prospective colleges or when Mark wishes to represent his journalist skills to peers or prospective employers, the portfolio is the basis from which they share themselves. It is from their portfolios that they pull together their work and the basis by which their work is assessed in a variety of contexts.

Assessment Using Portfolios vs. Standardized Testing

The benefits of portfolios are most apparent when what portfolios afford is compared with what seems to be traditional practices, especially the imposition of a narrow range of standards. The following chart summarizes the differences in assessment processes and outcomes between portfolios and standardized testing practices:

Portfolio	Testing
•Represents the range of reading and writing students are engaged in;	•Assesses students across a limited range of reading and writing assignments which may not match what students do;
•Engages students in assessing their progress and/or accomplishments and establishing on-going learning goals;	•Mechanically scored or scored by teachers who have little input;
•Measures each student's achievement while allowing for individual differences between students;	•Assesses all students on the same dimensions;
•Represents a collaborative approach to assessment;	•Assessment process is not collaborative;
•Has a goal of student self-assessment;	•Student assessment is not a goal;
•Addresses improvement, effort, and achievement;	•Addresses achievement only;
•Links assessment and teaching to learning.	•Separates learning, testing, and teaching.

Portfolios in the Classroom

We do not expect any two classrooms, nor any two students, to have the same portfolios. Portfolios should grow from the students' work, interests, and the projects and activities pursued by the class. Here are some "snap shot" descriptions of some classrooms that may give you a sense of the ways in which portfolios have been implemented across a variety of classrooms and age groups.

A Primary Classroom in Westerville, Ohio

In Westerville, the primary classrooms are literature-based with a great deal of emphasis upon writing. Shared book experiences, lots of different kinds of writing activities, conferencing, and projects are commonplace. Over the course of the year, students accumulate in their folders stacks of their own writing, response journals and other materials. Portfolios that showcase their special work become part of the classroom life as soon as the students have projects from which to select. Students develop and use their portfolios in a variety of activities:

- Sorting through their projects to decide what they wish to keep as "special";
- Noting why they think each of the projects selected is special;
- Collecting comments from friends and the teachers as to why they think different pieces are special;
- Sharing the range of their work and their comments with classmates, teacher, and parents;
- Deciding future goals for themselves with teacher guidance.

Each portfolio consists of a large folder for each student that is placed in a key location in the classroom so that the students have easy access to them. Students sort through them, select materials to go in and out of them, share them with their parents, classmates, and visitors and use them to help them decide upon future learning goals. These portfolios represent the work students do across time and serve as the catalyst and basis for self-assessment.

In previous years, such products were not gathered together, and the teachers rather than students assumed responsibility for assessing the gains that were made and the goals that were set. Portfolios set the stage in Westerville for expanding what was assessed and initiating student involvement in their own self-assessment.

Over a six month period of time, this second-grader developed a portfolio with a variety of carefully-selected work to reflect on and share with others.

Prior to Portfolios

Students were assessed on products, and teachers decided both achievement and future goals.

With Portfolios

Teachers and students assessed effort, improvement, process, and achievement across a range of work as well as the students' own ability to assess their progress and set future goals.

Self-assessment is pursued directly and indirectly by the Westerville teachers. Periodically, students are encouraged to select materials for their portfolio, conference with classmates about their selections, write book jacket kinds of comments about different pieces, and look over their work for purposes of reflecting upon what they had learned and wanted to learn.

Why I Chose This Piece	What I Learned	My Future Goals

On many occasions students share their work with their peers, selecting pieces they like or want to celebrate or just to compare them with others.

In conjunction with these self-assessments, the teachers at Westerville grade students, but this is done in partnership with the child and includes a consideration of effort, improvement, and process. It does not involve comparisons with other children.

Elementary Classroom, Upper Arlington, Ohio

Mark Carter, who is with Upper Arlington Schools, set up portfolios in his informal literature-based fourth grade classroom somewhat differently. At the end of every quarter, Mark's students select from their reading (journal entries, reading logs) and writing (projects, stories, etc.) those that they wish to place in their portfolio. While pulling together these materials, the students write an evaluation for each piece selected. During portfolio conferences with the teacher, the students develop their future goals.

Other students, the teacher, and the child's parents help in the selection of these materials and discuss with the child what they have achieved. In Mark's class, assessment is a collaborative effort. Assessment becomes a celebration of effort and improvement and a forum for teachers, children, and parents to consider future goals rather than simply to give the student a grade.

At the end of class projects, the class also pulls together a class portfolio—a place where the students and teacher gather together the projects and materials that represent experiences of the entire class.

Middle School, Columbus, Ohio City Schools

Chris Cassidy, a middle school teacher, uses a portfolio approach in a reading/writing classroom that focuses on the use of short stories, anthologies, and other materials. The classroom features several shelves filled with paperback trade books, magazines, and comic books. Along the back of the room is a large bulletin board with individual portfolios decorated and displayed with strings. There is a portfolio for each of the more than 100 children Chris sees every day. The desks are arranged in groups of twos and threes.

Chris uses a clipboard and checks off the names of each student as he sees their writing homework, and he holds spontaneous conferences with students during the check-off process. The portfolios in this classroom have a section for rough drafts and one for finished work. Students work with each other to revise and edit works in progress. At the end of each term the students share in the choice of which writings will be evaluated for their semester grades. Students agree to criteria and make suggestions about what grades they feel they deserve. Final grades are ultimately decided together.

This middle school teacher found a way to manage portfolios for over 100 students across several periods.

High School: Advanced Reading/Writing, Columbus, Ohio City Schools

In Carol Neutzling's class there are more portfolios than there are students. Each student has at least one working portfolio, which includes their drafts and notes, as well as one showcase portfolio for selected finished pieces. Each student's portfolios are different in both appearance and content. They represent the efforts of individual students as well as the outcomes of these efforts.

One kind of portfolio is the showcase portfolio, for which the students decided what they wanted to include and what their portfolios might look like. They decide how to showcase their work as well as what to showcase. One student, for example, showcases her work in a folder. She includes work dating back to when she was in elementary school.

The students in Carol Neutzing's classroom also have portfolios that they refer to as working portfolios, for work in progress. As the name implies, these portfolios include working copy, drafts, notes, comments from conferencing, the student's own self-evaluation, and so on. Each portfolio represents the processes students enlist and the responses students had as they read and wrote in response to different short stories and novels. They represent the history of reading and responding to selected stories.

The benefits are impressive. They afford students the opportunity to review what they have done and are doing, including their strategies, to formulate their assessment of their progress and to represent their effort, progress and process to others. For the teacher they offer a basis for conferencing, observing, assessing, and evaluating the student's processes, progress goals, and self-evaluations. For example, Neville's working portfolio includes her notes, reactions, drafts of responses, comments from both the teacher and peers reacting to her work as well as her own self-evaluative comments in response to *Fahrenheit 451*.

These high school students developed several kinds of portfolios. The top portfolio includes samples of the student's work from elementary through high school. James' portfolio includes a computer paper timeline of his life with photographs and even an airplane ticket that relate to different letters, poems, reports, and stories he has written both inside and outside of school. The two bottom portfolios include a rich assortment of school work and songs the students have written.

While portfolios can take various shapes and forms, they share a common philosophy—namely, users of portfolios believe that we should value what it is students are achieving and all that they are doing. In reading and writing, this entails valuing process as well as products, effort as well as outcomes, improvements as well as achievements, and diversity as well as standards. For example, when a student in Carol Neutzling's class represent her work, she displays her working portfolios as well as her showcase portfolio. She represents the thinking she did by sharing her drafts, responses, revisions, self-evaluative comments and the like. From these artifacts process as well as product and effort as well as achievement are apparent. To afford a wider glimpse of her abilities, working portfolios on other topics might be studied along with her showcase portfolios. For instance, by looking through her showcase portfolio you could attain an appreciation of the range of writing on different topics, for different audiences and purposes.

Portfolios in a Computer-based Classroom across Subjects

Computer technology offers a platform for students to create and integrate texts and images (both still and animated) using a variety of software, as well as to present their multimedia-based efforts in a dynamic, open-ended fashion.

In a similar fashion, Richard Tracy and Sheila Cantlebary have begun having their students pull together a showcase portfolio from the various computer disks representing their work in all subjects (math, science, English, and social studies) at the end of the year. A novel feature of their portfolios is the inclusion of a user guide. The user guide introduces the portfolio, explains how it is organized, and includes the basis for selecting material and self-evaluations. Tracy and Cantlebary work in a rather unique environment where students have immediate access to computers and various software (word processing, desktop publishing, spreadsheets, etc.). In their classes, which are usually team-taught, students complete numerous projects and assignments involving real-world problem-solving. Prior to using the portfolio, the students' work was often cleaned from their disks to make space for next year's work. As a result of the introduction of portfolios, their work from year to year no longer disappears but is retained for reflection, self-evaluation, and comparisons with later works.

Pursuing Portfolios

Over the past three years, we have been in more than fifty classrooms in which students and teachers have implemented portfolios. The results so far have been most encouraging:

- Students from kindergarten to college appear empowered, enthralled, and appreciative of the opportunity to develop, share and reflect upon their portfolios.
- Students take ownership of the portfolios and have a richer, more positive and expanded sense of their progress and goals as readers and writers across time.
- Assessment becomes collaborative rather than competitive.
- Parents are engaged in seeing first-hand what students are achieving. As a first grader suggested, "My parents were flabbergasted at how much I had done and grown."
- The literacy activities that students pursue along side of school (e.g., hobbies) or outside of school (e.g., leisure time reading and writing, songwriting) have a place to be represented in school.
- Teachers obtained a richer, clearer view of their students across time.
- Teachers negotiated a view of the student that is more fully informed in terms of what each individual child has achieved.
- Teachers have available to them the records or receipts of what students are actually doing.
- Teachers have a vehicle for pursuing assessment practices that are student-centered and focus on helping the learners assess themselves.
- Administrators have a vehicle for pursuing audits of classrooms and individual performance that represents what their students and classes are doing.

These portfolios can be used as a check upon the validity of other test results or as a means of creating benchmarks or school portfolios that are kept for the student across the school years. In one of the schools where we were working, a teacher was able to appeal the decision to retain a student when she was able to show the inconsistency between the test results and the student's portfolio.

Portfolios are likely to be a far richer source of information about a student's literacy achievement, progress, and ongoing development than other, more formal sources. Besides, portfolios have the potential to contribute to everybody's understanding of the student's ongoing learning in ways which are positive and grounded in reality. Our studies suggest that students, teachers, and parents develop in their understanding of their strengths and needs in ways they would not otherwise develop.

Chapter 4

Features of Reading and Writing Classrooms

Certain characteristics are becoming more common in classrooms. In a number of classrooms, teachers have developed a collaborative approach with students and have made specific opportunities are available for students. More and more teachers are establishing process reading/writing classrooms in which students are given multiple opportunities to interact with print, to choose the material they read, to collaborate and communicate with each other, to write often, to use literature for a variety of purposes, and to engage with assessment of their own progress.

Connecting Literacy Experiences with Students' Lives

In recent years we have become increasingly aware of the shortcomings of our schools not only for minority students, but also for disenfranchised individuals and groups such as students whose families are in lower socio-economic groups and individuals who do not easily "fit" into the school's social community.

As students move through the grades, an increasing number of minorities begin to fail whether or not their progress is assessed by traditional means or by numbers of dropouts and absenteeism. The problem is not limited to minorities; rather, it affects all of our students.

Student failure seems closely related to shifts in their attitudes and views of themselves as learners. In Columbus City, Ohio Schools, for example, surveys of students' views of themselves shows a decline beginning with middle school. Likewise, the National Assessment of Educational Progress surveys suggest that there are very able students who choose not to engage in reading and writing activities.

Reasons for this failure and disinterest may be tied to existing schisms between schools and communities. For many students school-based literacy activities seem too removed from their own experience. John Ogbu, an anthropologist, suggests that some black male students regard school assigned literacy experiences as requiring them to compromise themselves.

For these reasons and others, we encourage teachers to ask themselves how they can connect in-school literacy experiences with their students' experiences outside school. Teachers may take their consideration several steps further by asking:

- How might we encourage students to incorporate their out-of-school reading, writing, and other uses of literacy into their portfolios?
- How might we engage students with literacy experiences that connect their personal lives to academic work?
- How might students be encouraged to use literacy for self-expression and/or community change?

Several teachers have succeeded in helping students connect literacy with their lives, including individuals such as Paolo Freire and Ira Shor. Eliot Wigginton related literacy to his Appalachian students' lives with the launching of the Foxfire books. William McGinley and Daniel Madigan have pursued community-based writing projects with inner-city Detroit fourth graders. In conjunction with our portfolio research, several teachers included student work done outside of school. These activities included a class project exploring ways to assist younger students with dealing with the drug problem, cooperative work ventures with home and community-based groups such as churches and clubs, and letters, rap songs, and videos the students had produced independently.

1. Provide multiple opportunities for students to interact with books

Teachers in elementary classrooms, middle school classrooms, and high school classrooms are providing a stimulating reading environment by allocating time for books to be read and discussed aloud, for students to read and respond to readings independently, and for students to read and interact with books of interest in small groups. Accordingly, classroom collections of reading materials are becoming wide enough to provide reading for a variety of interests and levels. Teachers are also allotting time for students to write about and to talk about their reading experiences.

In one fifth grade classroom the teacher has spiral notebooks for each child. These spiral books are used as literature journals. Students are expected to make three entries in the journal each week. The journals are discussed during regular individual reading conferences. Occasionally she gives her students topics to write about, but most frequently students choose how to respond to the reading they are doing. During individual reading conferences the student shares his or her journal entries with the teacher. It is during this time that the teacher provides direction and responds to the students' thinking about the book.

Oftentimes students respond to parts of the book that the teacher would not have thought to ask about. In this way the students are free to have an individual reading experience that is personally relevant and still have someone that can monitor and enrich their thinking about texts they are reading.

Shared book experiences, drama, and other response activities can be enlisted to bring students into a greater level of awareness of issues, values and the interrelationships between plot, setting, and character values in literature. In English classrooms at the high school level and in middle school and elementary school classrooms many teachers not only share books aloud but also encourage students to share their own writing and reporting, thus honoring their own endeavors as authors. Students' expanded interaction with books not only provides them with information but can also generate the emotions that become catalysts for students to initiate their own explorations. Many times students develop a personal reaction to a book and find they want to share this.

Opportunities can be made for students to use books for a variety of purposes. This may mean that teachers will introduce many books and stories on many topics across genres. Some teachers in elementary classrooms have students using literature across the curriculum. Many books are brought into the classroom by the teacher and by students that support a topic of study. In one classroom the teacher had more than a hundred books displayed in different interest areas around the room that all supported the "nature" theme the class was investigating.

Accordingly, students in reading and writing classrooms generate work that reflects thought, ownership, and personal relevance. When students are attempting to showcase themselves as readers and writers they can do so by drawing from work they have generated in response to a rich and varied classroom environment.

2. Provide opportunities for students to talk about a variety of topics.

Work times in reading and writing classrooms reflect a commitment to collaboration between students. Students interact with each other while completing their work. They may have conversations about topics of their own choosing: selection of pieces for their portfolios or some of their future goals. These conversations can be the catalyst for new reading and writing topics. Student participation and collaboration means that stimulating ideas are presented by each member of the classroom. These ideas enrich and deepen student thinking and are reflected in the improved quality of student writing.

Teachers form book groups around student interests and allow students to talk about issues, characters, or events that are of interest to them. Students share stories, books, and their own writing and are asked to discuss each of these events. These valuable interactions allow for self-assessment opportunities. Students gather other perspectives and are more likely to make informed decisions. These collaborative experiences dovetail effectively with using portfolio, and may actually be key to a successful and creative portfolio process in the classroom.

Making a switch from a teacher-talk classroom to a student-talk classroom, however, can be difficult. As Carol says about her transition, "Turning over perceived teacher responsibilities is very difficult. Teachers want to select the gems, revise the papers, grade the essays, and make all the assignments. But the obvious result has been excitement—the student's and my own."

Carol has experienced that when students begin to be listened to and when their interests are sometimes the topic of classroom investigation, conversation, and writing, a new energy and level of involvement is created.

3. Provide opportunities for wide variety of writing.

At every grade level students are being given more opportunities to write about topics and issues of their own choosing. The amount of writing opportunities for younger students has increased dramatically. In one kindergarten class students began writing on the first day of school. The classroom teacher had developed an effective nonthreatening reading/writing workshop. Students can write about one of the many events that have happened at school or at home, or they can use the time to look through books or do extensions from a book the teacher has read. There are many choices so students are not forced into uncomfortable situations before the teacher feels the child is ready. Many of the students represent their thinking by drawing pictures and making a label for the picture. Several kindergarten teachers have successfully incorporated writing portfolios into their classrooms. Kindergartners often comment on how much their writing is improving during the times they are adding new things to their portfolios.

Journals often serve a variety of functions in classrooms. In many classrooms students have several different journals. In one fifth grade classroom that utilized portfolios, students wrote in writing journals, poetry journals, and literature response journals.

Reading-writing classrooms have become environments which afford students multiple opportunities to engage in a variety of literacy events.

The writing journal was used during writing workshop. Students wrote on topics of their own choosing most of the time during writing workshop. Four kinds of writing most often appeared in these journals: fictional stories, personal narratives, informational pieces to go along with a theme being studied in the classroom, and writing about assigned topics. During individual conferences with the students, the teacher listened to students share their current writing. The teacher provided assistance that was helpful for the individual as well as monitoring the amount and kind of writing each student was doing. If the teacher noticed that the student was only doing expository writing the teacher suggested that the student attempt a different kind of writing and provided the help and support so the student felt comfortable making a transition to writing in a different form.

Students were encouraged to write in their poetry journals—spiral notebooks—on a daily basis. The classroom teacher read poetry daily, usually at the beginning of writing workshop. Students began writing workshop by writing something in their poetry journal: an idea for a poem, or list of topics, a response to a poem read by the teacher or by another student, or a tentative line or two.

Students made two entries into a literature journal sometime during the week. Most of the time students responded to their reading by writing about topics of their own choosing. Two or three times a month the classroom teacher presented a question or issue for students to respond to in their journals. The assignments pulled together important issues from the class read-aloud or from a book group experience.

The project journals focused on writing across the curriculum. During a study about animals, students kept notes from guest speakers, movies and filmstrips, and from readings they had completed on an animal about which they had chosen to become expert. A section of the project journal was designated as an observation section. The students, under the teacher's direction, created a mini zoo in the classroom. Students kept detailed journal entries about the animals they were studying, which included snails, lizards, snakes, salamanders, newts, and turtles. This project motivated students and provided many interesting experiences to write about. Some of the writing that was generated was chosen by students to go into showcase portfolios to illustrate an understanding of scientific research, detailed record keeping, and the depth of information students learned about a certain animal.

Journals for this particular classroom, then, were a major source of material for students' portfolios. As students searched for material to showcase, they would peruse their various journals en route to making selections.

4. Interactive collaborative assessments.

Teachers may not realize the extent to which their assessment is collaborative or could be more collaborative. Many teachers have developed ways to share the responsibility of assessment with their students. In these classrooms students are being asked to think about the quality of their own work. By encouraging students to engage in self and peer evaluation teachers empower students to take control of their own learning. When students help determine the criteria for assessment they can make reasonable decisions about the quality of their own work.

By engaging students in self-assessments students learn they are ultimately responsible for their own learning. It is in this area that portfolios are so powerful. The atmosphere many teachers have created in their reading and writing classrooms increase student involvement in assessment. As students are asked to take on more responsibility for selecting topics for their reading, planning theme work, choosing reading material, and deciding on the criteria for projects, evaluating individual efforts is meaningful and purposeful to students.

A fourth grade teacher states that, "Students save work in their portfolios. Children see progress. It's obvious. Both the student and I know the work they have done and how it was done. We both can see the strengths and areas to work on."

In classrooms that utilize portfolios, teachers and students are analyzing portfolios to determine many facets of student work including versatility, effort, achievement, growth in use and understanding of a thoughtful process, and progress over time. A reasonable message is given to students about learning and performance by utilizing performance assessment procedures that value the work of students in a variety of areas over an extended period of time. Students learn that quality work takes time and that input from others, while in process, facilitates depth of thinking.

Teachers are finding that, through using a reading/writing portfolio, students can become involved in collaborating and reflecting on their own work. Through this process student strengths and needs become more visible to students and to teachers.

Portfolios, in reading and writing classrooms, help students to:

- Make a collection of meaningful work;
- Reflect on their strengths and needs;
- Set personal goals;
- See their own progress over time;
- Think about ideas presented in their work;
- Look at a variety of work;
- See effort put forth;
- Have a clear understanding of their versatility as a reader and a writer;
- Feel ownership for their work;
- Feel that their work has personal relevance.

In our research with teachers and students we have found that students prefer portfolio assessment over more standard forms of assessment. One student put his feelings about using portfolios this way, "It was a chance to show your writing and express how you are. And to let people know your real character...like, you know, if you're imaginative or creative."

Students have become very involved in collecting, comparing, analyzing, and selecting work that will represent them in their portfolio. These students enjoy the more collaborative role offered them in their classroom.

Developing Sensitive and Informative Procedures

In reading and writing process classrooms there is an abundance of data generated by students. By collecting and analyzing this data, teachers are finding appropriate direction for instructional interventions for individual students. The data reveals student strengths as well as areas where the student repeatedly gets stuck. Changing the focus of instruction to individuals has opened opportunities for teachers and students to communicate about matters of importance that facilitate individual progress.

Interacting with students in the process of becoming more mature writers and readers generates a valuable source of information that is necessary for planning meaningful interventions. Interaction, either in impromptu conversations, scheduled conferences, small group reading or writing meetings, or listening to students converse, is an important characteristic of many reading and writing classrooms.

Conferencing with students, with portfolios present, allows teachers to develop a broad picture of the child based on different tasks that have occurred over a period of time. In conferences, assessment and instruction are inseparable. This process honors students as collaborators as teachers and students share their thinking with each other.

Through careful observations, detailed analysis of student portfolios, reflections, and systematic interactions with students, teachers become more sensitive to the information that is available that clarifies a student's strengths and needs. Instructional interactions formulated with a clear meaningful purpose for the child help teachers and students succeed in the classroom.

Three crucial elements are present during instructional contacts with students: the child, the teacher, and the portfolio. Having the portfolio in front of the child helps focus the conference on the student's ideas. Through discussion portfolios used in conferences can be a vehicle for discovery and enlightened thinking. Drawing examples from the child's work to emphasize a particular idea is a powerful teaching aid.

Student As Decision-maker

Positive reading and writing classroom environments have emerged in recent years that support and encourage a high level of student participation. Students are being encouraged to choose their own writing topics, read books that have personal relevance, and develop criteria for assessment. In these classrooms, students generate their own writing and reading for a variety of purposes, sharing and discussing their own reading and writing, and engaging in self-assessment.

Portfolios that contain carefully selected samples of work are meaningful to students in classrooms where they have a high level of personal involvement. A high school student shared that he "liked portfolios because they gave students a chance to prove themselves. Some of the students can really write!" His teacher, Carol Neutzling, feels that, "Students have enjoyed being a part of planning their own reading and writing. Seldom have they been given the chance for so much input about requirements for an assignment or for the standards of evaluation."

The involvement many students are experiencing in reading and writing classrooms empowers them to share in decision-making in their classroom. Carol feels that her students have developed a strong sense of ownership for their work since their responsibilities have increased. Her students have an opportunity to write and read pieces that are meaningful to them, review each piece, compare and contrast their pieces, and decide which pieces represent their best thinking, effort, and versatility as a reader and a writer. Students are empowered to choose pieces to place in their showcase portfolio. Carol and her students will work together to evaluate the portfolios. Their evaluations of the portfolio will eventually determine the student's grade in the course.

Reading and writing classrooms like Carol's provide students an opportunity to reflect on their own thinking, discuss readings, and generate a variety of writing that represent the depth of student thinking and their level of writing proficiency.

This is Chris Cassidy's first year using portfolios in his classroom. He has involved his students at a level of real importance. During this year his teaching style has changed to allow students a collaborative role in deciding writing topics, criteria for assessment, what pieces will be evaluated. Chris has his reading/language arts classroom arranged in a workshop atmosphere. He works diligently to motivate and actively involve his students. He involves them by requesting, listening to, and responding to student input and interests. This makes them active partners in shaping some of the content curriculum.

Chris said that before he adopted a process reading and writing model to guide his instructional thinking, he relied on the English skills text. He feels that his classroom used to be very teacher-directed. As more and more information emerged about encouraging students to write for purposeful reasons, Chris adapted his teaching style. "I had to make provisions for students to be at different stages on writing assignments and personal writing. Portfolios are the hub. Students touch, look at, and discuss their pieces. They have ownership. They share and interact. The physical structure of my room changed to accommodate student conferencing."

Both Chris and his students have taken on new roles. A new level of activity fills Chris's room. He enjoys the new professionalism. "It is a challenge to incorporate curricular goals into a creative classroom," he says about changing instructional role. Chris knows his curriculum and helps individuals and small groups accomplish curricular goals through their own writing.

Overview of Teacher and Student Roles

Carol and Chris have adapted their teaching and in the process they have empowered their students. There are different roles or expectations for behavior in their classrooms. These new roles facilitate the implementation and use of portfolios. There is no question that both Chris and Carol are the leaders in their classroom. They both set the tone for thoughtful classroom interactions and have developed an environment that encourages students to take risks. The chart below outlines some important roles in operationalizing a portfolio approach to reading and writing assessment.

Teacher Roles	Student Roles
• Provide a well provisioned classroom;	• Choose writing topics;
• Plan for student involvement, interaction, and input in classroom activity;	• Choose reading material;
• Provide time for assignments that encourage decision-making, drafting, reflecting, discussing, reading, and responding;	• Organize, maintain, and accept responsibility for reading and writing portfolios;
• Provide instruction and modeling of expectations;	• Involvement in self and peer assessment;
• Assess student process, effort, progress, and achievement, as well as products;	• Collect, analyze, compare, and select writing and reading samples;
• Help students manage portfolios;	• Collaborate with others to understand personal strengths and weaknesses;
• Collect and analyze student work samples;	• Set goals.
• Develop an interactive style of teaching;	
• Use information gathered from interactions with the child about their portfolio to guide instructional direction;	
• Use analysis and samples to report to stakeholders.	

These roles are being lived out in high schools, middle schools, and elementary schools across the country. Teachers believe that the classroom environment is important to facilitate student interest and learning. Teachers are provisioning classrooms with reading materials that interest students, learning areas filled with hands-on materials to stimulate thinking about a theme that is being studied by students, reference books, computers for word processing and creative desk top publishing, and a variety of paper and writing utensils to support student writing.

Large budgets certainly help; however, building rich environments is more of an attitude than a money issue. A spirit of inquiry cannot be purchased. Students can bring in collections of books and magazines from home and immediately the environment begins to take on a new tone, a tone that says to the students: What you think counts here.

In reading and writing classrooms that encourage student involvement teacher plans are changing also. Teachers are planning more ways for students to take active roles by allowing more time for students to draft, reflect, and have conferences with teachers and students about real questions and dilemmas students face as readers and writers.

Along with the changes in classroom structure, the way teachers are viewing assessment is changing also. By using interactive teaching methods teachers like Chris and Carol are deepening their understanding of their students with every contact. Instruction and assessment are occurring concurrently.

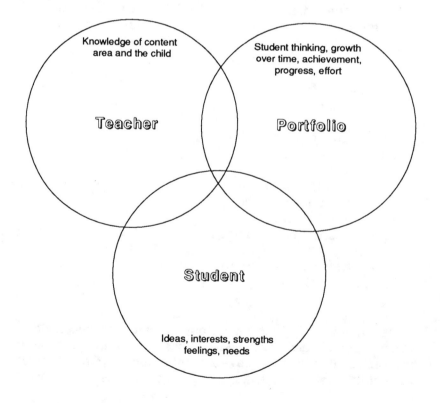

Furthermore, portfolios of student work provide opportunities to clarify instructional needs, reveal student strengths, celebrate student thinking, value student interests, take into account effort, and engage the student in deliberations and conferences that help the student understand their own achievement and progress.

Portfolios offer teachers a sensitive, flexible procedure by which to assess student classroom work. Student portfolios in the same classroom will undoubtedly be vastly different. Each student will showcase pieces that represent their own thinking, interests, and strengths.

Portfolios may have one particular focus or may showcase a wide variety of student work. It may be that you have a student who loves to write poetry. That student may want to keep a poetry portfolio. The portfolio could emphasize the ideas the student wishes to express as well as his or her understanding of form and poetic devices. In this way one specific focus can be emphasized and deliberated about closely. A portfolio that has a particular intent provides students a medium in which to represent their thinking and understandings about a particular aspect of reading and writing. This portfolio may be an aspect of a larger more inclusive reading and writing portfolio.

Reading and writing portfolios contain samples of student work that demonstrate the changing understandings students have as they mature as readers and writers. For example, one fourth grade teacher has her class keep reading and writing portfolios that are representative of the work they do during the year. In her classroom, students may keep finished pieces they have published, evidence of wide writing including a variety of forms, pieces that are evidence of growth and development over time, a list of books that have been read including date completed and genre represented, written responses to literature experiences, and pieces that represent the child's writing process, including writing in different phases of completion. To develop reading and writing portfolios, she plans carefully so classroom activity supports the generative and reflective work students need to be doing so adequate samples of work are available to represent effort, progress, versatility, quantity of work completed, and capabilities.

Portfolios vary from class to class. In a fifth grade classroom students keep portfolios that showcase what they are capable of in reading and writing. Their portfolios contain examples of their progress, achievements, process, strategies, efforts, versatility, and self-evaluations for both reading and writing.

In all classrooms though, portfolios go beyond mere folders or collections of student work. Items in a portfolio are reviewed, compared, analyzed, and possibly reworked.

Items in portfolios are chosen by students to represent

specific aspects of themselves as a reader and a writer. The items not only chronicle the development of a student's thinking but also show the result of instructional interventions. Through a wide collection of student work assessment is able to be descriptive and continuous.

An exciting feature of using portfolios for many teachers is that they are actually monitoring the effects of their interventions each time they conference with a student. Their suggestions can be tailored to be effective with each student. Program analysis occurs in a consistent, integrated fashion.

Contexts for Learning

In many reading and writing classrooms students have been empowered to share in developing the planning, criteria, and evaluation for their reading and writing work. Teachers feel a new level of excitement from exercising their professional judgments to increase student's ownership, enjoyment, and progress in their school work. They especially enjoy that students are more involved and responsible for their own learning and that students are more informed about classroom expectations.

It is exciting to think that portfolios of students' authentic work are being carefully developed, by teachers working hand in hand with their students, and sent on from year to year supplementing or even replacing standardized measures. Portfolios, containing authentic pieces of work, carefully chosen by students, are providing students an opportunity to showcase their talents.

One high school student sums up these feelings about his writing portfolio:

> I prefer portfolios because looking at the portfolio you can see where you started out, see how much you have improved since then. I write better now. I express my feelings better. I'm more organized and my mechanics are better. I learned that it is good to venture into different types of things. You can write different types of papers you never thought you would be able to do. Of course it was hard but with a little assistance from classmates and the revision processes we used made things a lot easier.

The Classroom Environment

The process of writing can become extremely personal, especially as students are encouraged to write poetry, fiction, and personal narratives. Students who are experiencing difficult personal lives (living in a dysfunctional family, for instance), students who are members of devalued social groups (ethnic minorities, children from poor families, children with disabilities, and so forth) and students who feel that their lives are not acceptable to the teacher or the classroom community may experience a great deal of difficulty writing or allowing others to view their writing. They may not want their parents to see their writing, or they may choose less personal pieces to put into a portfolio because they are not ready to share significant information about themselves. They may have difficulty accepting feedback from their peers during workshop sessions or during informal conferences. It is critical for teachers to recognize and support students' rights to both privacy and acceptance from the community, to set by example high standards within the classroom community for support and appreciation of diversity, and to find ways of helping these students explore writing processes in ways that reduce personal risk or exposure. Students helping to set criteria to determine the expectations for the quality of work; students involved in making decisions about topics for reading and writing; assessments that involve students as collaborators; a supportive atmosphere; interactive teaching, conferencing, and attention to individual interest and needs—are elements of reading and writing classrooms that are making it possible for students to have meaningful learning experiences.

Chapter 5

Getting Started with Portfolios

Observations in many classrooms have helped us understand that meaningful, useful portfolios must reflect what is sensible and important to you and your students. Key concepts and helpful suggestions will be discussed in this chapter that will help you put portfolios into operation in your classroom. The intention of this chapter is not to lay out "THE" way to get portfolios established in your classroom; it is, rather, to help teachers help students to discover themselves. Writing and reading offer places for students to discover their thoughts. We hope that each child is able to develop a personal collection of writing and reading that has significance for the owner. Understanding your students as human beings and helping them see a connection between school and real issues in their lives is an important springboard portfolios can provide.

Classroom teachers of all grade levels have followed similar procedures for creating portfolios in supportive classroom contexts. To establish portfolios you and your students will more than likely need to make provisions for the following: establish ownership, save representative work samples and provide a storage area for work collections, brainstorm elements that may be in reading and writing portfolios, communicate with parents about portfolios, discuss reading and writing to help students discover their thinking and recognize features of stories and of quality writing, introduce the portfolio concept to students, provide guidance and time for students to compare and select pieces for their portfolio, facilitate self-evaluation, establish a review process, and plan for portfolio conferences.

Establishing Ownership

When students read and write on topics of their own choosing and then select samples from their work to showcase themselves they come face to face with their thoughts, feelings, and strengths as a reader and writer. An important belief of the authors of this book is that portfolios lose their effectiveness if they are institutionalize. We use the term "institutionalize" to refer to the use of portfolios in terms spelled out by outsiders. If students lose control of their own work, portfolios become just another assignment. A key is to introduce and use portfolios so that they remain the students' property. In this way students become an important force in the classroom. The ground work will be set for students and teachers to work together in an atmosphere that helps students to take an active role in school issues that affect their lives.

In some classrooms, the student work folders belong to the teacher. The teacher assigns all of the reading and writing tasks, grades all of the assigned work, and chooses the pieces that are to be placed in student folders. A primary reason for the portfolio, however, is to engage the student at a new level of involvement. Teachers who accept students as collaborators begin to see and understand their students in a new light. Teachers who use portfolios express that they become aware of and more sensitive to their students' strengths and needs and are able to provide personalized instructional support for students.

Benefits exist for students as well when they assume ownership of their work. Students begin to recognize their own strengths and needs, and assessment becomes a reasonable process to them. They begin to understand what they want to write or read, what is expected, how to improve, and they begin to recognize the power of their own and other's pursuits. One student said he liked evaluating his portfolio because, "It showed the student how the student has improved, and what the student could do to keep improving." Comments like this epitomize the benefits of taking the mystery out of assessment by including students in the process of assessment with classroom work that is under their control to compare to criteria they have established, to reflect on, to analyze, to make sense of, and eventually to develop understanding of and control over.

Save Work Samples

Many teachers have students keep folders of their own work. It has been traditional for teachers to keep folders of students' best work to share with parents at conference times. Working with students to help them save a wide variety of their reading and writing work is an important first step teachers can take in getting portfolios started.

Shirley, a third grade teacher in Columbus, Ohio City Schools, has her students keep writing folders, math folders, and project folders. Students keep their own work in these folders while they are working on a specific project. At the end of the week Shirley collects, reviews, and returns the folders containing work the students have compiled during the week. She has had a chance to check it for completeness and accuracy and intervene with those students who are having difficulty. Students search through their folders and keep best pieces in a Best Work Folder. She and her students have started a collection of the students' best work.

Sherry, a fifth grade teacher in Upper Arlington, Ohio, keeps every piece of writing her students do during the year in one drawer of her file cabinet. Each child has a folder, made by folding a 12 x 18 piece of construction paper in half, in which to store his or her writing when it comes down from displays. At the end of the year, she asks her students to choose three pieces from their folder to put in a cumulative writing folder that is kept in the child's permanent record and is added to each year the child is in school. Sherry has established an effective way to save her students' finished writing.

Kathleen, a first grade teacher in Upper Arlington, Ohio, tapes students' reading three times each year as a part of her collection of student work to illustrate the students' growth as readers. She also keeps student art work and writing that are responses from book experiences in a reading folder along with the list of books the students have read. There is a place in the folder to note strengths the teacher has observed during reading conferences as well as goals the student and teacher decide on together.

Each of these teachers has established a procedure to collect student work that represent certain aspects of the students' growth. Initially, you and your students can begin by designating a place for students to keep their finished work. In most classrooms students and teachers share in the process of deciding what to collect. It is important to keep a wide variety of work so students actually have work to choose from to place in their portfolio that represents their thinking, their level of achievement, their versatility, and their progress over time.

A well provisioned portfolio can be a powerful tool that can be used to share with parents and others. At this point it is not necessary to limit the collections students make to only the "best" work. These broad collections become a pool of work from which children can draw throughout the school year to showcase their reading and writing for particular reasons.

Elements in Portfolios

The list below represents possible elements that reading and writing portfolios could contain. It is not our intention to suggest that all of the following items should be represented in every student's showcase portfolio. There are elements in the list that could be important for primary students, middle school students, and high school students to include in their portfolios. Since reading and writing growth is a continuous event there will be some overlap of development represented by student portfolios across grade levels. The list or menu is not inclusive of every possible kind of work that could be placed in portfolios. The list is meant to give teachers an idea of items that could represent aspects about a student as a reader or a writer.

There are both process and product elements in the menu. Process elements reveal how the child goes about reading and writing tasks. The emphasis is on strategies used and the child's awareness of the strategies being used. Process items reveal individual differences in how students go about their reading and writing work and encourage awareness and thoughtful reflection on the importance of the journey. We would offer a caution about process artifacts. For some students, an overemphasis on process—a formulaic approach to planning or revision for example—may hamper their ability to create the new material.

Product elements are evidence of the understandings that students have about reading and writing that can actually be put into operation. The goals of reading and writing programs include helping students respond to their reading, apply what they learn, communicate with an audience, and understand other authors' attempts to communicate. Product elements are examples of students' responses to what they read, projects that accompany the reading and writing they do, as well as attempts at utilizing their knowledge. They reveal students' strengths and needs at communicating with a variety of audiences in diverse forums.

The list of items are representative of items that students can collect and place in their portfolio to showcase themselves as readers and writers. Process and product items obviously serve both purposes. That is, a piece that reveals a student's development of a paper also is evidence of their achievements. Likewise, reading and writing elements also overlap. There are reading elements that are expressed through writing about reading experiences.

Some possible elements for reading and writing portfolios
- Projects, surveys, reports, and units from reading and writing
- Favorite poems, songs, letters, and comments

- Interesting thoughts to remember
- Finished samples that illustrate wide writing
  - persuasive
  - letters
  - poetry
  - information
  - stories
- Examples of writing across the curriculum
  - reports
  - journals
  - literature logs
- Literature extensions
  - scripts for drama
  - visual arts
  - written forms
  - webs
  - charts
  - time lines
  - murals
- Student record of books read and attempted
- Audio tape of reading
- Writing responses to literary components
  - plot
  - setting
  - point of view
  - character development
  - links to life
  - theme
  - literary links and criticism
- Writing that illustrates critical thinking about readings
- Notes from individual reading and writing conference
- Items that are evidence of development of style
  - organization
  - voice
  - sense of audience
  - choice of words
  - clarity
- Writing that shows growth in usage of traits
  - growing ability in self-correc-

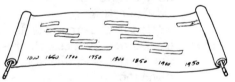

tion, punctuation, spelling, grammar, appropriate form, and legibility
- Samples in which ideas are modified from first draft to final product
- Unedited first draft
- Revised first draft
- Evidence of effort
  - improvement noted on pieces
  - completed assignments
  - personal involvement noted
- Self-evaluations
- Writing that illustrates evidence of topic generation

Hopefully, the menu will stimulate your thinking about the kinds of reading and writing events that occur in your classroom that could assist students in showing and discovering themselves as readers and writers. Collections will undoubtedly differ from classroom to classroom and from student to student depending upon teacher and student interests, cultural background, grade level, and many other variables.

These elements are examples of student work that can aid teachers and students to develop an understanding of student thinking. Reviewing these items with students helps teachers and students discover new directions for inquiry, new ideas, and an accurate appraisal of students' strengths.

Collecting work is not unusual. However, using the collected work for self-analysis is an unique feature of the portfolio assessment process. Representing students as readers and writers in the portfolio allows the students' continuous literacy development to be accurately documented. Whether students are in elementary school or in college, saving samples of their work is necessary if they are to have the data to reflect upon, to facilitate their understanding of their own strengths, needs, and development.

Parents as Partners

When students are involved in generative classroom work, fewer work samples are available on a daily basis to go home for parents to see. It takes time for students to write meaningful stories or to generate a thoughtful response to a reading experience. Once you start collecting reading and writing work students generate, even that will not be going home on a regular schedule. Anticipate that parents may be concerned about the lack of work coming home from school. If you are making a transition from a classroom where lots of work went home on a daily or weekly basis toward a classroom that collects and savors student work, you will need to communicate that change to parents. It will be necessary to develop new procedures to keep parents involved and informed.

One method of keeping parents informed about classroom activities is to write regular parent newsletters that chronicle classroom events. One newsletter could be sent to inform parents about a development of writing and reading portfolios in the classroom. A parent newsletter to inform parents that work is being kept at school so that students can develop a broad collection of their work will help parents understand and feel involved in the process. Inform parents that work samples from folders will come home regularly but that you would like to have the work returned on the following day.

Of course teachers could always have an open house to share portfolios. Parents could come in at a designated time with their child. The child could present his or her portfolio to their parents. When the child was finished they could leave.

Dear Parent,

Today your child is bringing home his or her "Writing Showcase Portfolio." Much time and thought has gone into the selection and evaluation of the pieces in it. They are still in the process of being refined, but we want to share them with you at this time. You will notice there are 5 pieces of your child's writing in the portfolio. Below is a detailed description of how this Showcase Portfolio was developed over the past 2 months.

We began by discussing what a portfolio is, using the example of an artist, model, photographer, or even teacher, having a collection of their best work to show to prospective employers.

Each child selected what they thought their five best writing pieces were so far this year. They have saved all of their writing throughout the year in a folder, so they selected from that, as well as many pieces which were kept on their own computer data disk. Then, they wrote why they selected each one on a green 4x6 card. The first time they did this, they tended to write personal reasons: "I like it" or "This is my favorite." After we discussed further the purpose of portfolio, that is, to showcase examples of their best work and share them with others (friends, teachers, and parents), they realized that they needed to point out specific examples of good writing skills. Thus, the comments changed to such things as, "I used good paragraphs," "This report was focused on the subject," "I had good word usage when I used many different words," or "The poem rhymed." We talked about the criteria used in holistic assessment of their writing, and I gave them a sheet which describes papers ranging from 1-6. (This is in the pocket of their Showcase Portfolio).

Next, the children added features to their portfolios which made each one unique. Many put in a Table of Contents, illustrated the pieces, wrote an "About the Author" page, decorated the cover, wrote a page about why they liked all their pieces, etc.

After the initial self-assessments, I wrote a comment on a yellow card about their portfolio. They proceeded to refine their evaluations and selections. Very few children changed their selections, although I encourage them to be constantly considering replacing a piece in their Showcase Portfolio if they write something better. Just before each grading period, we will thoroughly re-evaluate the portfolios. I would like to see more variety in the selections in some portfolios, however the choices are strictly made by each child.

Today when your child shares this very special folder with you, s/he will ask you to evaluate one piece which s/he has chosen to be looked at by others—you, me, and a friend. I would like to suggest some guidelines for you to follow as you write your assessment on the 4x6 orange card attached to that piece of writing. First and foremost remember to be positive; only write about strengths of the piece. This is not the time to be critical. You shouldn't be pointing out spelling errors, wrong word usage, the fact that the piece could be shorter or longer, etc. Hopefully, the piece is as near to "perfect" as your child is capable of at this time, for s/he selected it as an example of their personal best. I might know of better work they've done, but this is not my portfolio. Remember, also, that this is only ONE of your child's

many, many stories, poems, letters, reports, reading responses, etc. Be aware, too, that this has become something extremely personal, special, and a source of pride to your child.

I have been putting off sharing the Showcase Portfolios with you until they were in a finished form. However, the longer we work with them, the more clear it becomes that they will never become "finished."

Because these portfolios are never a "completed assignment," the children can see the progress they are making as writers. When they remove a piece, they have to tell me why the replacement is better. Of course, it is important for you and I to know the child's strengths and weaknesses. That is how I am able to guide them in becoming better writers. But it is even more important for the child to know his or her own strengths and weaknesses. Self-assessment is a very effective means of doing this. Thank you for taking the time this weekend to sit down with your child and talk about their Showcase Portfolio. Personally, I think it is much more indicative of their progress than that "O" or "S" which was written by me on their report card a few weeks ago under "Writing." Please be sure the portfolio is returned on Monday.
Jan Beagle, Barrington Elementary School

Sincerely,
Jan Beagle

Jan Beagle, a fourth grade teacher in Upper Arlington, Ohio, sent home a parent letter that not only informed the parents about the portfolio process but also invited them to participate in the scrutiny of a student selected piece.

Examples of Letters to Parents

February 16, 1990
Portfolios

Normandy School
Dear Parent(s),

At open house I discussed our use of portfolios for the year. First, I would like to refamiliarize you with what we have been doing. The children collected their work done in reading and writing in a storage bin (accessible to them) in the room. Throughout the first nine weeks they shared the work with classmates. Toward the end of the first nine weeks each child chose three pieces that were special to him or her in some way. Finally, I met with each child. In the conference we spoke about why each of the three pieces was special, and I used this opportunity to help the student verbalize why one particular piece might be stronger than another. Weaknesses in areas were also noted and discussed. I believe strongly that these are critical opportunities for the children to evaluate their own finished pieces and to begin to verbalize their strengths and weaknesses.

We are all in a learning curve with this project, and as we repeat this process each nine weeks I am sure the benefits will increase.

A next important step with the portfolio is to share them at home. You are receiving two separate units with this letter. The larger set of items were those completed in the first nine weeks but not chosen by the children for their portfolio. These you may keep. The second set of items are the three special pieces.

I would ask that you allow your child to share his or her special pieces with you. I have attached a sheet on which I would encourage you to comment. It is imperative to a portfolio project such as this that you give your child lots of praise. If you see problems, realize these are being addressed in class. If you are concerned please feel free to contact me. Most important, I ask that you find only positive things to say about your childs work.

We will be repeating this process after each nine weeks and I feel sure that as concerned and involved parents I can count on your support.

The three special pieces must be returned by _____ so that we may keep them in our portfolio and compare our work as we grow throughout the year.

Thank you again,
Miss Fritschle

• • • • • • •

Normandy School
March 1990
Dear Parents,
    We are again sending home our portfolios to share with you. Please take some time to look over our three newest special pieces and find some positive comments to write down.
    The large set of papers may be kept at home. Please return the portfolio with two sets of special work.
    Thank you for your support and concern.
Miss Fritschle

● ● ● ● ● ● ●

    Teachers who invite parents to participate in celebrating the positive efforts of their children help parents gain a deeper understanding of the process of developing as a reader and a writer. It helps parents appreciate the strengths their children have developed as well as understand the need for the support and kinds of activities and instruction you are providing. Educating parents, through involving them in guided viewing of their child's work, gives them first-hand experiences that enable them to understand their developing child and the efforts schools are making to engage students in becoming full participants in their own education through expanding teacher and student roles.

Reflecting on Writing and Reading

    A feature of reading/writing classrooms is providing opportunities for children to share their work with their peers. Students who are older may be reluctant to share. It is still important to have upper elementary, middle school, and high school students share their pieces, although may be necessary to have students share their work in small groups or with reading/writing partners instead of in one large group. Authors have an opportunity to express their purpose in writing the piece, for all students need the opportunity to hear other students' comments about their writing.

    These experiences can broaden student thinking as well as provide insights about style, use of mechanics, and attention to audience. Reflecting on their work with other students becomes a vehicle for students to discover important ideas, explore new concepts, think in new ways, and refine their methods of communicating to different audiences.

    An ongoing chart can be developed as a way to record student insights about reading and writing. Student samples can be used as exemplars of a certain feature that students think is important to emphasize in their work. For example, if a student writes an expository piece that has well developed paragraphs the piece could be used as an example of that feature. The chart that is developed from the students' input becomes a menu of features that are characteristic of quality writing that the students recognize.

In a first grade classroom we were in recently, students had begun a chart of "What makes writing good." On the poster were student comments like the following:

exciting story
interesting pictures
use of . ?
funny characters
capitals
has a title
sounds like a story
like the story

This first grade teacher encourages the students to discuss the features they admire about Maria's work and her approach to writing.

If you have an overhead projector, it could be used occasionally to share visually a special piece with the class so it could be discussed in depth. Students could suggest features of good quality writing. Doing this by using a complete sample keeps the integrity of the piece intact. It is important to preserve the context as the features are only meaningful in the context of the whole writing sample.

Accept student's thoughts about writing. When we begin to understand what our students think, we can offer appropriate guidance that successfully facilitates individual progress. In some classrooms, teachers have asked students from other classrooms to share portfolios, discussing why they chose the pieces they did and their future goals. In some second and third grade classrooms, students complete self-assessment sheets. For example, the students in one class periodically review their portfolios, list what they have learned, and detail future goals. It's amazing how much they will list as they learn about themselves.

Students also need to have time to discuss reading they are doing. Like sharing writing, reading discussions can happen in a variety of forums. Teachers have had a lot of success having students discuss readings in small groups. Students that have similar reading interests can form discussion groups. Certain stories could be discussed in a whole class setting, while other personal readings might be best discussed during individually scheduled reading conferences.

Writing about literature experiences is greatly enhanced through peer and teacher interactions in a community of readers. Not only do students grow in their knowledge of books available to read, but they also have a chance to reflect on how the reading made them think or feel about a certain topic. Students can discuss the kinds of reading they do to meet certain purposes. As students share reading experiences, characteristics of various genre and literary features of stories become more clearly articulated.

Once students have a variety of samples and have generated ideas about criteria for quality writing and the uses and purposes of writing, they are ready to begin to apply that criteria to their own writing. Student comments, even at the upper grades, will not be as sophisticated as teacher comments. It may be that they focus on features of reading and writing that are not that important at first. Remember, they are just beginning to develop the tools necessary to think critically about themselves as readers and writers. Even at a beginning level, students can become engaged in the act of reflecting on their work. The very fact that they are becoming increasingly responsible for judging the quality of their own work enables students to take control of their own learning.

Introducing the Portfolio Concept

It is common in certain fields for students and professionals to have a portfolio that represents their skills. It may be that you could invite a local artist, a high school art student, or even a journalist to share his or her portfolio with your class. The visitor could be asked to share individual pieces and tell why they have been included in the portfolio.

For example, in one classroom the teacher introduced her students to portfolios through Amy, a high school art student who was willing to share her art portfolio. Her portfolio included a selection of her work in different media (sculpture, line drawings, screen prints, watercolors) as well as works in progress. In presenting her portfolio she shared her goals, self-analysis, and view of each work as well as the whole.

Explain to students they are going to create their own portfolio that will represent their very best thinking, effort, knowledge of process, problem-solving, versatility as a writer and reader, progress, and achievements. Discuss with them the possibility that they might include pivotal pieces as well as their best work and a range of documents that capture the breadth of their efforts as well as the trail of their progress.

Students might forget all of the things they have read or written. As a class, make a list of the pieces that have been written and read. Students may want to go through their work folders to help them recall each piece. When they are ready to begin selecting some of their work for a portfolio they should have an opportunity to see their collection of work. They may have forgotten that a certain piece of work is very special.

Students can decide, with the teacher's guidance, how many pieces should make up the portfolio. Some students may want to include everything, while others may not want to include anything. A reasonable number should be decided upon. For the first portfolio, most teachers we have worked with start with three to six pieces. Too few pieces may leave some students feeling all of their special pieces cannot be included, while too many pieces may limit the very important task of contrasting and comparing work that has been collected so a critical decision can be made about what to put in the portfolio based on a clear rationale for each selection.

All portfolios do not look alike. Some teachers use large artist's folders while others use pocket folders. Some others have had students keep their writing and reading portfolios on computer disk. Students who use disks often include a section on the disk that serves as a table of contents as well as provides directions for the order in which they would like pieces to be viewed. Portfolios can be designed to suit your classroom context best!

One Classroom's Concept of a Reading/Writing Portfolio

We have found that during the selection process students

like to have comments from others regarding their choices. As students make selections, encourage them to work with a friend or two and to share pieces of work at home. Some teachers ask students to choose portfolio partners. These students comment about which pieces they think are the better pieces and explain their reasons for their decisions. Of course, the final decision will remain in the hands of the owner of the portfolio. Having students give comments to a friend not only clarifies and supports a decision but in many cases provides additional reasons why the piece should be included. These added insights help the owner scrutinize his or her work from a broader perspective.

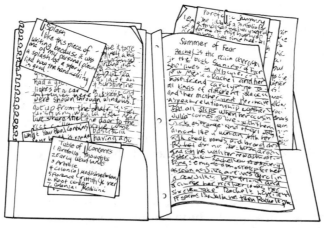

The left side of this portfolio is devoted to writing, and the right half to this student's reading responses. The student has attached index cards with self-evaluative comments.

Students who need more guidance in developing their portfolio than others may benefit from direct assistance from the teacher. Pinpoint several strengths in their writing and ask them to find similar strengths in one other piece. Students may lack confidence in choosing their best work. Provide the support necessary for them to succeed and remove the support as they increase in their ability to choose for themselves. Students in learning disabled classrooms have successfully used reading and writing portfolios with a teacher that helped make the purpose and method of portfolios clear to them. An art of teaching is giving the additional direction when necessary.

Portfolios may take on special individualized focuses. Some students may see themselves as budding poets or as award-winning fiction authors. Their portfolio may overemphasize these forms of writing. Encourage the feverish author to "follow the dream" while at the same time recommend that the student develop another section of the portfolio for other pieces as well.

Students often personalize portfolios by including an interesting design on the outside, using certain colors of paper for their finished pieces, including an elaborate table of contents, producing interesting pieces using desk top publishing software, or adding autobiographical pages. This variability should be celebrated. It is one sign that students are genuinely interested in their portfolio. One high school student wanted to develop a theme for his portfolio. He stated, "When I put my portfolio together I wanted to show my personality, my thoughts, and present issues that I feel strongly about to give other people something to think about." Allowing students to personalize their portfolios can bring out a personal commitment like the one this student has expressed.

Apple Classroom of Tomorrow (ACOT)
Student Handout on Portfolios

Creating a Portfolio
Portfolio (It. portafoglio, Fr. portare to carry (fr. L.) + foglio leaf, sheet) 1: a hinged cover or flexible case for carrying loose papers, pictures, or pamphlets 2: (fr. the use of such a case to carry documents of state): the office and functions of a minister of state or member of a cabinet 3: the securities held by an investor: the commercial paper held by a financial house (as a bank).

Why create an ACOT portfolio? What are its purposes?
Your portfolio will include samples from the following areas:
I. Writing samples
   A.   What are some of your strengths as a writer?
   B.   What are some of your weaknesses as a writer that you will work on next year?
   C.   Which piece represents your best writing this year?
   D.   How have computers influenced your writing?
II. English/Social Studies project samples
   A.
   B.
   C.
III. Science/Math samples
   A.
   B.
   C.
   D.
IV. Keyboarding early and later samples
   A.   What were your most successful experiences with your early typing?
   B.   How have you improved your keyboarding skills?

C.   How have your keyboarding skills changed?
Words per minute?
V.   Miscellaneous (Your own files)
A.
B.
VI. Guide

Create a printed "user's manual" for your disk. This should include an introduction that explains how your disk is set up. Be sure to tell your audience what software they will need to run your files.

Include a statement on why you selected each piece for your portfolio. You may describe your effort, frustrations, pride, growth, and interest connected with the particular selection. You may also include information about who helped you and what you would change if you were to redo the project.

Notes: This project will be worked on at home and at school. You should have two disks, one to turn in and one to keep.

Self-evaluative Statements

While each piece of work is being considered, ask students to think about their reasons for possibly including the piece in the portfolio. Some teachers have asked students to write their reasons for inclusion of an item on a 3 x 5 card and then paperclipped the card to the actual piece.

Example of 3x5 Student Evaluation Cards

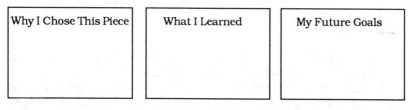

| Why I Chose This Piece | What I Learned | My Future Goals |

With younger students, and more than likely the first time older students are asked to develop their thoughts about their work, it will be difficult for them to make comments about form, style, clarity of text, logical content development, or other sophisticated features. Comments like: "I like this piece because it's my favorite" or "This writing shows how good my handwriting can be" may tend to dominate the first round of portfolio comments.

However, after students gain experience with comparing and contrasting their work and become more familiar with explaining features in their own and other's writing, more substantial comments will develop. Comments will change, certainly with older students, to include such things as: "This piece is special to me because it is about the last time I saw my grandmother"; "The information included in the piece is thorough and sufficient for the reader to make a judgment about the points presented"; or, "The piece was focused and did not meander from the topic." As students are able to make comments such as these about their essays it is clear that they are developing the skills to act as a reflective writer and to use writing to meet diverse purposes.

Example of a Portfolio Peer Review Sheet
From Apple Classroom of Tomorrow

What to do: Browse through three of your peers' portfolios. You must do the person directly across from you or one person assigned by the teacher. Choose two other portfolios you would like to review.

Look at three entries. Identify the best or the unique features of each entry and explain how those features enhance the students' work. You may also make general comments about the way the portfolio and user's guide is set up.

PORTFOLIO ONE: NAME_____

PORTFOLIO TWO: NAME_____

PORTFOLIO THREE: NAME_____

Reviewing Portfolios

After students have assembled the pieces of work that will go into their first portfolios, it is time for you as their teacher to read and analyze them. Initially, you may want to jot comments on individual "Portfolio Review" sheets about strengths and needs that you notice. This way you will end up with an individual overview sheet for each student. During this reading try not to compare student pieces to outside criteria. Simply view each student's portfolio as it is. Allow yourself time with the portfolio so a picture of the student emerges from the collection. Respond honestly using your knowledge of writing and reading, class expectations, and your growing understandings of the strengths and needs of the individual student.

Reviewing portfolios is time consuming. This is another reason for limiting the number of pieces that go into portfolios. Your written comments should be kept as brief as possible.

Comments on your review sheet may range from concerns about the range of books and compositions pursued, interests, effort, approach (planning, use of resources), collaborations, self-evaluatons, improvement, as well as strategies used to cope with difficulties. You might also approach aspects of style and versatility, recognizing a strong personal voice or tremendous efforts. You can note the extent to which the student is using literacy to reflect upon issues and to pursue personal interests. You may wish to keep track of your comments—in a tabbed binder, for instance—and use them as a basis for reports to parents and others.

While reading the portfolios you may want to use a list of features and a checklist to consolidate issues that occur across portfolios. In this way you can see strengths and needs of the entire class in a condensed form. On the checklist you could place the students' names along one column and label the rows with a range of options that you may select from for noting the progress of different students. Your list will probably contain differing features for each student.

Some teachers make a checklist of issues about reading and writing that they have noticed in many portfolios. You could record, for example, which students use reading and writing for a variety of purposes, reading experiences in various genres, or which students are and are not successful at expectations and at this time. This list can provide information for teaching points for individuals, for small groups and for entire class mini lessons. In this way you are continually informed, through a highly valid procedure, about the developing strengths and needs of your students.

Portfolio Conferences

Insights from portfolio reviews are used several ways. They can be used in student-teacher portfolio conferences. Begin the initial portfolio conference by asking the child to present or share the portfolio with you. Allow the student to retain control of the portfolio. Tailor individual comments to provide the reinforcements the student needs as well as the instruction that would be helpful for a student to improve as a reader or writer.

You can do this by selecting one or two teaching points to emphasize during the conference. Ask the student what he or she thinks are the strengths of the portfolio. Point out what you think are the positive aspects of the portfolio. Comment about the agreement you share with the student about a particular evaluation of a piece. Together, the student and you may end the session creating goals for the student to work on during a certain period of time. When the student feels a particular goal has been accomplished you can ask the student for new priorities or refer to your analysis of the portfolio for new teaching points to emphasize.

Regular reading and writing conferences may take from five to ten minutes. A scheduled portfolio conference may last from ten to twenty minutes. Time for conferences emerges as teachers and students play out new active roles in the classroom. Since in reading/writing classrooms student activities such as working on their own writing, conferencing with peers, reading for an intended purpose, and discussing literature in small groups are valuable uses of classroom time, the teacher is able to hold individual conferences.

You may only have one, two, or three conferences a day, depending on how involved the conference needs to be and on the other activities you want to facilitate in the classroom. It usually takes longer than a week to complete all the portfolio conferences for one class. If you teach in a middle school or in a high school it is impractical to consider having more than one hundred conferences. You may want to rotate classes for which you hold conferences or have small group conferences. Teachers may also facilitate peer portfolio conferences. Try rotating conferences using various suggestions until you find a system that is right for you—that is, one marking period have individual conferences with one section, peer conferences with another section, and small group conferences with a third section.

Classmates and teacher engage in a conference. The student uses them as a sounding board for his work. The teacher offers input for the student and notes his progress.

A Report on the First Year of Portfolio Assessment

The Apple Classroom of Tomorrow[SM]

Excerpt from a report by Sheila Cantlebary and Richard Tracy

...We both became increasingly interested in the portfolio for assessment idea. We were fairly discouraged by...comments on the futility of standardized testing with which we, for the most part, agree. We see portfolios as a way to provide richer information for ourselves and for the students. Portfolios can, we hope, "fuel learning" in a way standardized tests cannot....

We have been bothered by the [institution of] additional standardized testing. We doubt that these measures will show much of what our students have accomplished. Instead we have preferred to amass a kind of rich collective portfolio with a wide variety of student-produced materials. That is how we want our program evaluated....

We were constantly reflecting during the pilot...We didn't want to be too restrictive in our directions to the students since this was exploratory. Besides we weren't even sure what we wanted to do.

When we introduced the project, the students were passive. There were few questions and little feedback. We tried to make them aware that they were partners with us in the research... The students did seem engaged from the beginning and began immediately to initialize disks and to browse through their files....

Many students seemed to be taking pride in what they were doing. Jodi got excited about completing a "miscellaneous" project she'd been working on during the year, a Hypercard stack on her favorite rock group. She ended up staying after school for two hours Friday night so she could have access to the scanner as she continued working. As she left she announced that even though her birthday was the next day, she was going to work all day on her portfolio. On Monday she told us that she had stayed up until 3:00 a.m. compiling her portfolio.

In her user's guide Jodi reflected, "you are reading this project. I used many things to do this, I think this is what they call a mass-media project. This is the project I enjoyed most this year. I put everything that I was proud of or not so proud of on one disk. Looking at this portfolio I see where I could have done something different and in the future I might choose to do a similar project that way. Another thing the portfolio did was to give me an excuse to make my Triumph stack [a rock band]; it might not have gotten done."

The biggest problem for all the students seemed to be the lack of time and the fact that they had not saved work from earlier in the year. We asked them to write comments and suggestions. Many were insightful and helpful...

The students had particular interest in each other's [portfolios]. This gave them an opportunity to share their peers' special interests. Most of these files were created at home. They included short stories, data bases, poems, games, original student art, and student-enhanced clip art. Several students commmented about Jenny's file entitled "Stars 30's, 40's, 50's." Michelle wrote, "I looked at a list of her stars that she likes...and she has them listed along with some important facts about them. It was interesting to browse through!"

The portfolio assessment was indeed valuable in our year-end evaluation and was included as part of our final exam. We definitely want to continue to use portfolios next year. We need to share our work with the other teachers in the program and involve them in the planning...

We're not completely certain how often to do portfolios. If we only do one near the end of the year, we will make the assignment early and have checkpoints along the way. The sharing process needs work. We'd like to allow time for multimedia presentations. Then, too, perhaps we can require students to share their work with a parent and have them include comments. We need to make the expectations for the user's guide and reflective statements clearer. We want to allow room for creativity there but also to make sure certain information is included. A reading component needs to be added. We need more than just a list of books, though. Perhaps we could have students keep a reader's journal as part of the portfolio. Some students would like the option of turning in not only a disk, but also a folder of hard copies. Others would like to use HyperCard for the entire portfolio...

All in all we feel good about the results of our first attempt at student portfolios. We are convinced that they are worthwhile for students and for teachers. We are getting a real picture of student progress, effort, and attitudes. We hope they may prove to be of interest to parents also. We are even hopeful that if we can refine this, other educators may find our work worthwhile as they, too, consider alternate means to student assessment.

Summary: Using Portfolios

1. Respect students' ownership of their work.

2. Students and teacher collect samples of student work generated in a classroom context that is supportive of student interests, decision-making, and collaboration. Establish a safe place to keep student collections (folders, notebooks, a drawer in a file cabinet, etc.).

3. Invite parents to be involved in the portfolio process. Students can share their writing with parents to help

parents understand the kind of reading and writing that is taking place in the classroom. A regular parent newsletter can help keep parents informed about classroom activity.

4. Facilitate class discussion about establishing showcase portfolios. Explain to students that they are to choose pieces (best pieces, pivotal pieces, companion pieces, etc.) that represent their strengths, interests, versatility and effort and trace their development. Discuss aspects that make reading and writing special. Place their ideas on chart paper so students can refer to the list to assist them when they write personal reasons for including pieces in their portfolios. Use student exemplars when possible to illustrate aspects of reading and writing. Help students recognize these elements in their own reading and writing.

5. Discuss different elements that could be included in their portfolios. Again, place their thoughts on chart paper so they can refer to it as they put their portfolio together so students do not forget pieces they have in storage.

6. Assist students in selecting work for their showcase portfolios. During this choosing process students have an opportunity to analyze and compare their pieces. They can make explicit why they have chosen certain pieces. Initially, your students may need help making choices about what to select. It may be helpful to work with students to develop guidelines about what to keep. Discuss saving pieces that show what the students like or can do well, such as special topics, favorite books, range of writing/projects, lists of books read, responses to readings, and so forth.

7. Ask students to write their reasons for including each piece in their portfolio. These pieces can be dated to help students recall dates completed. Work could be labeled on a 3 x 5 card stapled to the work that tells the strengths the piece shows or other reasons for its being included in the portfolio.

   The writing selected for a showcase portfolio can be discussed with peers. Students can be encouraged to write an evaluation of their portfolio, which could include a response about the process used in selecting and finalizing their showcase portfolio. Students can do a table of contents and even organize their portfolio into sections (reading section, writing section, pieces in process, etc.).

8. Take time to review the portfolios by yourself. Allow each portfolio to reveal its own specialness. Reflect on what your goals have been. Are the students meeting these goals? Write a few comments on a portfolios review record about the strengths and needs you notice about each portfolio. If it would be helpful, create checklists to facilitate instructional interventions as well as to keep track of student accomplishments.

9. Update portfolios at regular intervals. As collections of student work grow, students will have a more difficult time narrowing their choices for their portfolio. When portfolios are updated, students can include work that illuminates progress. Some teachers update during particular times in the year while other teachers and students revise portfolios continuously. Decide, with students, on how many pieces should be included in each successive revision of the showcase portfolio. This will force students to compare, analyze, and select carefully.

10. Students may share their portfolios with other students at a class meeting and with their parents at a scheduled open house. Students who are willing could read selected samples aloud. As a class, have students work with the teacher to decide on criteria for portfolio evaluations. Students can be assisted to engage in peer assessments that are fair, helpful, compassionate, and insightful.

11. Use portfolios to discuss aspects of student work with parents and district personnel. A district-wide portfolio assessment program could be established to replace other less valid forms of assessing student understandings.

This process will help you establish portfolios that reflect important issues while at the same time respect individual classroom goals. Showcase portfolios are a tangible collection of student interests, thinking, effort, versatility, progress, accomplishments, and skills. To use portfolios effectively, interact with your students. This process helps you get to know your students on a personal level. Portfolios help promote good teaching and observing habits because they facilitate a thorough understanding of reading and writing, as well as how your students progress as readers and writers. We believe portfolios enhance your reading and writing program by making the child and his or her strengths and needs more visible to child and to you.

A key concept in using portfolios is to give students as much responsibility in maintaining them as they can handle. The students learn valuable organization skills and they develop a sense of ownership.

One middle school teacher feels that the most significant change in his students since using portfolios is the value they now place on their own reading and writing. He also feels his students have a sense of ownership in the process of "school" as they become more involved in helping decide topics for writing, in helping form assessment criteria, and in selecting and evaluating their writing and reading.

Chapter 6

Sustaining Portfolios

Meaningful Assessments Occur over Time

$\mathbf{T}$oday, more than ever before in education, teachers are asked to be accountable for student achievement and progress in reading and writing. Regardless of grade level taught, teachers need to develop an accurate appraisal of each student in their classroom. It is also important for each student to develop a sense of his or her achievements. We have found that teachers and students who critically analyze the contents of reading and writing portfolios over time will develop a comprehensive understanding of achievement and growth that is rooted in the students' actual classroom performance.

Consider, if you will, some of our students' reflections on themselves as readers and writers in conjunction with reviewing their portfolios:

"I saw how my writing has improved over the past three years. I write better now. I express my ideas better. I am more organized and my mechanics are better. I have learned quite a few things about myself that I hadn't noticed before until I started comparing my writing from eighth grade to this year. I've noticed how my attitudes toward different topics have changed, such as topics that affect our society like drugs and teenage pregnancies. My opinions toward those things have changed."

"Maybe I'm a better writer than I give myself credit for. I have a lot of writing. I never realized how much I writing I had done until I pulled it together for the portfolio or enjoyed writing because I have a lot of stuff that I had done out of class. I never realized I wrote about things that really affected me, like I had written an article about things that really helped me out."

These students have learned that it is important for them to analyze and assess growth over the time. They comment on being aware of the quality of ideas, organization, mechanics, effort and amount of writing, the motivations for writing, and their own personal development as human beings.

Teachers who use portfolios feel there are advantages to using portfolios over other forms of assessment. The chart below illustrates what three teachers feel are advantage of portfolios after using portfolios in their classrooms:

Teacher A
- Students share work with other students.
- The teacher is involved with what kids actually do.
- Students have more control—must be more responsible as they manage their own portfolios.
- Classroom is more responsive to students.
- Students learn they are doing this (reading/writing) for themselves.

Teacher B
- Students can see their own progress as they compare and contrast pieces.
- Teacher sees work done and how well it is done, as well as how it has improved.
- Errors and strengths are right there.

Teacher C
- The obvious result is excitement – students' and teacher's.
- Students have enjoyed being a part of the planning. Seldom have they been given the chance to give so much input on requirements for an assignment or for the standards of evaluation.
- Students have pride and increased sense of authorship. Writing partnerships have increased this pride.
- Evaluation sheets on papers have positive results. They make conferences more efficient. Evaluation sheets also provide impetus for self-evaluation. They must also assess strengths and weaknesses as well as assign grade.

Utilizing reading and writing portfolios in assessment makes a difference for students and for teachers. They make a difference because teachers have made an effort to sustain their use over time; analyze and understand student achievements, progress, and needs; and involve students in self-assessment. During the process of sustaining portfolios, teachers use ongoing student collections to provide insights for instructional planning and discuss and reflect with students upon the characteristics of the portfolio as a whole.

Updating a portfolio on a periodic basis is a rewarding experience. It represents a mix of rediscovery and self-evaluation along with the struggle to decide what to include, exclude, reconsider, highlight, and propose.

Updating Portfolios

Teachers who use portfolios in their classrooms afford students time to perodically update their growing collections, time to reflect on their work, assistance in deciding what criteria to apply in their decision-making, and opportunities to conference with them and their classmates.

In several classrooms (elementary, middle school, and high school) teachers asked students to prepare updated portfolios each nine weeks. Deciding on the number of items that would be in the portfolio was an important group decision.

In a fifth grade self-contained classroom, students kept year long showcase portfolios. Portfolios were divided into two sides: a reading part and a writing side. The teacher discussed the contents with the students so they were aware that there were pieces that could easily go on either side, depending on what reason the piece was placed in the portfolio. For example, Lindsay chose a piece of writing about frontier life for her writing side because it was a well organized expository piece of writing. She could also have put the piece in her reading side as it illustrated her ability to synthesize information from her readings. The first quarter students agreed that at least three pieces be placed in each side of the portfolio. The second quarter the teacher and students decided each side of the portfolio should contain three to six pieces.

To provide additional support for student's teachers ask students to share items with several friends or with an editing partner. Students are given class time to read and comment on each other's selections for their portfolio. Up to a week is given for students to peruse, analyze, and decide what pieces are to represent their best work. Parents are involved in some classrooms. Students are encouraged to share several pieces with their parents to get their input about the strengths of each piece.

Several teachers who use portfolios do not take a specific week to focus on portfolios. They have their students update portfolios throughout the year. Each time a student finishes a piece of work he or she is asked to decide if it should go in the showcase portfolio. The teacher and the student discuss the piece's merits and compare it to others in the portfolio to see if it offers new features that would enhance the portfolio.

Illuminating Students With Portfolios

Each time portfolios are updated, students are asked to determine features to notice as they analyze their own writing and reading work. These features are added to a continuing list or chart kept by the classroom teacher. For older students features can be categorized into appropriate areas that exemplify strengths students have as readers and writers. Caution has to be taken here or students will begin to believe that teachers are looking for certain "skills" only. Student samples should be viewed as a whole and in that context certain elements are judged, by teachers and students, to be used correctly and effectively. It is important that students are aware that the essence of the piece, its purpose and meaning, are more than just the sum of its parts. It is the orchestration of those elements that can occur in infinite patterns that is at the heart of reading and writing.

Many qualities of writing and reading have been generated by students as they study and discuss their own and their classmates' work. It is the process of generating and perceiving these elements over time that helps students develop their own reading and writing. Examples of student-generated ideas about features to notice in their own reading and writing are listed in several categories below.

Sharing involves revealing work to and pursuing reactions from other students.

BREADTH OF READING EXPERIENCES

    Reads across content areas while working on projects

    Reads stories

    Reads poems, songs, and a variety of other material

TYPES OF WRITING

    Reports

    Essays

    Letters

    Journals

    Reflections

    Documents

    Other

USES READING AND WRITING

    To solve problems

    To pursue projects (everyday, community-based, classroom-based, home-based, school-based)

    To communicate with others

    To influence or affect others

    To enjoy

    To engage in "lived-through" experiences

    To make new connections and discoveries

To check on ideas or satisfy curiosities
To learn about people and places
To learn how things work
To gather one's own thoughts
To improve self
To reflect on own life

STRATEGIES

Planning
Constructing ideas
Dealing with difficulties
Reflecting
Sharing

RESPONSE

Explores new possibilities
Writes about a variety of story elements
Expresses in depth ideas about a reading passage
Relates readings to personal experiences
Summarizes readings
Synthesizes from a variety of sources
Compares and contrasts

STYLE

Strong voice
Appropriate voice
Attention to audience
Careful word choice

DEVELOPMENT

Logical paragraphs
Organization
Depth of thought
Coherent story line
Clear focus
Well formed sentences
Variety of sentences
Use of paragraphs
Beginning middle end

USING CONVENTIONS

Appropriate spelling
Proper capitalization
Correct punctuation
Legible handwriting

SELF-EVALUATION

Thoughtful analysis of efforts, achievement, and shifts/improvements
Makes comparisons
Assesses improvement
Sets future goals

READING AND WRITING FLUENCY
>   Reads with appropriate expression
>   Uses strategies effectively and efficiently
>   Adjusts reading to meet different demands of
>   texts and purposes
>   Effectively reads and reworks own writing

The items above represent developmental ranges of characteristics of reading and writing that students can illuminate as they reflect on their own strengths. Students can use a single piece of work to represent multiple features in their portfolios. As they reflect on a piece and write about its strengths they often recognize several elements that are embodied in the piece.

Sometimes students may be encouraged to take a piece that may have not been included in their first portfolio and either rework it or reevaluate it so it is significantly improved and use it as a sample in a later updated portfolio. In this way students can be encouraged to revisit ideas at a different time with a fresh perspective. Helping students reflect on their work and develop a critical stance about the quality of their own work can be accomplished through conferences with them. Students can develop their ideas on how to improve a piece and learn to recognize their strengths.

Possible Criteria for Assessment
From Student Writing Portfolio, Columbus Public Schools

Look for growth in these areas:

Content
- finding a subject
- narrowing a topic
- having a controlling idea
- collecting specific information on that subject
- supplying appropriate and significant information
- ordering and presenting content to meet a reader's needs
- using transitional devices to accommodate the organization of ideas

Style
- presenting the information with clarity and grace
- using appropriate diction for his/her purpose
- using variety of sentence structures

Mechanics
- following the customs of spelling, usage, punctuation, and capitalization
- following the custom for a manuscript: margins, paragraphing, neatness, and legibility

Portfolios Provide Information for Instructional Decisions

Student collections that have been assembled over a period of time present an unmistakably clear image of what students have actually accomplished. Each portfolio will be different. The contents of the portfolios will represent topics the students have found interesting as well as the process they have used to create their products. Long term portfolios help teachers understand the ideas and concepts students are consistently struggling with, those that the students have mastered, and the individual developmental process of becoming a mature reader and writer.

By analyzing the collections teachers are able to make informed decisions about instructional interventions that provide the timely assistance students need to gain confidence and competence. Teachers who analyze portfolios over time are able to get to know their students, what makes them excited, what interests them, and how they perceive themselves.

Once a classroom reading and writing program emphasizes student choice in a wide variety of reading and writing experiences, supplies ample time for students to read and write, and encourages self evaluation, the teacher is able to provide meaningful interventions that are based on the students performance.

Conference for Portfolio Assessment
From Student Writing Portfolio, Columbus Public Schools

Do:
- Build on what the writer has done and encourage the student to recognize what he[she] can do and what he[she] has done, then see what more he[she] would like to do to grow as a writer;
- Praise the writer by becoming involved in the specific writing. Praise by describing the effects specific techniques have on you as a reader;
- Listen carefully to the student's perception of what are successful strategies for his or her writing. Respond to the writer's concerns about his or her writing;
- Reinforce writer's terminology whenever you discuss the piece of writing and what aspects on which to concentrate for the future;
- Limit goals set by the teacher and writer so that students can attend to and accomplish them;
- Discuss how the writer performed to produce this particular piece of writing. Include both the pitfalls and successes of this effort.

Don't:
- Bemoan what isn't in the paper or what is wrong with

what is there;
- Be judgmental about the writing so that you take over ownership in determining what is or isn't good writing;
- Overwhelm the student with too many objectives or things to consider;
- Take over the dialogue so that it becomes a lecture;
- Concentrate just on the product and not the process of writing.

Features of the Entire Portfolio

There are features of the portfolio as a total entity that students should also take into consideration as they are reflecting on and writing about pieces that go into updated versions of their portfolios. Later portfolios begin to reveal rich information about readers and writers that students can be helped to understand and orchestrate to illuminate all of their strengths. Individual pieces may be able to illustrate a student's control over a few important elements; however, the power of a portfolio is the accumulation of a variety of pieces that, taken as a whole, show broad and expanding control. A collection of student work reveals quite a lot about the personal characteristics of the student. Not only are a student's confidence, interests, and quality of thinking visible, but so are a student's power, versatility, effort, knowledge and use of process, self-reflections, and growth.

Power

Portfolios reveal the power of the readers and writers. The sheer volume of work they are capable of producing is what is considered power. A portfolio should make a prolific reader and writer visible, and students should be recognized and supported if they are avid readers and writers. As teachers, we need to be aware of the students who would literally carry on without us.

We all know students who read hundreds of books during the school year or write for their own enjoyment. These students have special needs. They may benefit from book suggestions and individual times to discuss their reading. Some students write volumes for their own enjoyment. They may improve their writing if they have a mentor who takes an interest in the stories or poetry they do on their own.

Teachers can provide guidance if they are aware of students' power and ask themselves: What special needs do these students have? What can I contribute to make their reading and writing experiences more meaningful?

Versatility

Over time, portfolios show the versatility of readers and writers. With the support and direction of a skilled classroom teacher students learn to read and write in a variety of experiences and opportunities that facilitate wide reading and writing. Teachers do this in a variety of ways. They choose topics to study that are of interest to students. For example, a class study about the sea captures students' imaginations and provides multiple entry points. Students read informational books on sharks, whales, or any other animal they may be interested in learning more about. Poetry books are shared and written. Students read fictional books about sea adventure and respond in literature journals. A newspaper may be started that focuses on problems that confront sea life. Editorials and articles are written.

During the course of the year many themes may be studied. The teacher can provide a balance of activities that give students opportunities to study a wide variety of genres. Students could read and have read to them realistic fiction, biographies, historical fiction, informational books, and fantasies. Students should have opportunities to write in a variety of forms, including poetry, expository, personal narrative, persuasive, and fictional stories. Students can be encouraged to build portfolios that show their versatility as readers as well as writers. We can help students to become aware of versatility as a goal by being aware ourselves of the kinds of writing and reading our students are doing and direct them to forgotten or neglected areas.

Effort

Effort is an important feature for students as they update portfolios. Students in high school classes and in elementary classes can keep reading and writing records to illustrate not only the types of books they have read but also the extra things they have done. Some students may read a book over and over again or they may work on a piece of writing, revising it several times until it is just the way they want it . They are different from the student who quickly finishes a task and never looks back. The introspective student may be willing to receive your thoughtful comments and certainly will need your reassurance.

It is important to help students value quality work. The portfolios that reflect the extra effort it takes to rework a piece until it is the very best the student can do should be recognized and celebrated.

Use of Process

Understanding how students go about their reading and writing task is also an important goal. Students can have pieces in their portfolios in all stages of completion to show how they go about different tasks. As students do so they can be asked to reflect upon their own process of reading and writing.

Teachers can ask themselves: How do students approach the reading and writing of different texts? How do students integrate information from various sources? Do students take notes or write summary passages about their reading? What is the nature of the students' self-reflective comments? How have students revised their writing? Have they adopted different perspectives? Have students reread their writing? Understanding how students go about reading and writing can help teachers make meaningful interventions that provide important information about how a task could be done more effectively.

Self-reflection

Many teachers who use portfolios in their classrooms have students write about the pieces they place in their portfolios. Student perceptions about their own reading and writing is an important aspect of student learning to consider before making instructional decisions. Often times students' comments reveal what is important to the student.

Students may place items in portfolios because of one aspect they have noticed or because of multiple reasons. Students may like a piece for personal or sentimental reasons; they may value the work for the quality of ideas or for their use of descriptive language; or writers may like their organization, mechanical skills, or their choice of topic. Likewise, readers value their work for a wide variety of reasons. An item may be placed in the showcase portfolio because it is a topic the student is interested in, an author the student admires, a familiar and favorite genre, a piece of writing about a text that expresses an aspect that is significant to the reader, or for a host of other reasons.

Understanding what a student is focusing on and how this compares to the strengths you see in portfolio samples can help you help students to see their pieces in a broader perspective. Since students are the ones being evaluated, it is important for them to understand what others are evaluating about their work.

Student Questions for Self-evaluation of Portfolio Writing
From Student Writing Portfolio, Columbus Public Schools

1. How does this writing compare with other pieces of writing you've written this year?

2. What makes a piece of writing good? Relate these "good" qualities to this paper.
3. At present, what do you feel are your strengths in writing? How does this paper reflect these strengths?
4. At present, what areas of writing give you the most difficulty? Are these difficulties reflected in this writing?
5. What qualities of this piece led you to choose it as your best?
6. Reflecting back on this piece of writing, is there anything that you now think you would do differently if you were writing it again?
7. What changes have you noticed in your process of writing?
8. What would you like to work on improving in your next piece of writing?

Growth

A strength of the portfolio concept is that it helps students, teachers, and parents see the growth and development that has been made. Many teachers and students have shared that the growth is "right in front of you."

Parents feel reassured when pieces from early in the year are laid beside pieces from the end of the year and the classroom teacher points out several areas in which their child has progressed. It is difficult for parents to see growth from only letter grades on report cards. Having concrete examples is a powerful tool to convince both parents and students that growth is occuring.

Monitoring for student growth also helps teachers assess their own programs. If teachers see several students struggling with similar concepts or neglecting certain aspects of reading or writing, they can add mini-lessons to help students overcome problems or broaden students' reading and writing experiences.

Using a Broad Perspective to Monitor Growth

Portfolios are a framework that provide teachers, students, and parents with information in an alternative process to standardized tests. They can help teachers develop clear expectations for students, actually decrease paper work, provide continued insights into students that enhance teachers' effectiveness, and help students take an active role in their own learning.

Measuring growth using portfolios does not exclude students from the process of assessment. Assessing students through portfolios reduces or eliminates test anxieties and provides a valid and reliable composite on which to base educational decisions. Using the student's actual classroom work provides actual data about how students perform on tasks that are important for their success in their classroom. Most importantly, teachers and students gain insights about where further instruction is needed. Many teachers feel that instructional contacts gain power as they focus on students and needs for success in the classroom away from test preparation.

Furthermore, a portfolio process of assessment protects students from biased tests and the misuse of test results. Students who come from all backgrounds can be assessed effectively by teachers through interacting with them on work that has been accumulated for analysis. Children who are poor test takers yet are capable students are not penalized by evaluations that focus on a variety of samples collected over a period of time.

Portfolios involve a partnership between students, parents, and teachers. It is a partnership centered on empowering students to assess themselves. For many teachers, this is a desirable goal. As one teacher states, "Turning over responsibilities to students is very difficult for me. I want to select their gems, revise their papers, and make all the assignments. The enthusiasm, pride, new skills, and new teaching methods generated by greater student involvement in revision and assessment of writing make this effort worthwhile."

Portfolio assessment positions students to learn about themselves at the same time as it places teachers in the position of being an assessment coach. Maintaining portfolios over the course of the year allows the teacher to learn about each student and therefore to become the critical link that supports and nurtures growth. In the portfolio process teachers are empowered and valued as professionals capable of making insightful instructional decisions. Through using knowledge of reading and writing development and instruction combined with knowledge about each student, teachers individualize and personalize interventions. Assessments, centered around a rich and varied collection of student work, are meaningful, continuous, and intertwined with instructional goals.

Chapter 7

Portfolios and Self-assessment by Students

An interesting trend in reading and writing instruction has been helping students become independent learners. Along with attempts to improve reading comprehension, educators have gravitated to ideas such as strategic learning and metacognitive control in hopes of developing classroom practices that help students achieve independence. In conjunction with the increased interest in teaching literature, self-selection by students and interpretation have been stressed. The increased interest in writing includes a great deal of emphasis upon student decision-making. Students choose the topic, make decisions about what to include and revise, and so on.

Despite the emphasis upon students as decision-makers, students still are forced to play what has become commonly known as the "game of school." They have learned that it is important to know what the teacher wants:

"How long should it be?"

"What do you want?"

"Is spelling important?"

"What counts?"

In most classrooms, the teacher decides what is "right" and "wrong," "exemplary" and "poor." It is the student's goal to anticipate and meet somebody else's (the teacher's) criteria.

It is unfortunate that most students hand in their papers or responses to the teacher because some of the most valuable "teachable moments" disappear. It is as if teachers assume an ordained right: the power to separate the wheat from the chaff. What is left forgotten is helping students learn to assess their own work.

Some people might excuse this oversight by claiming that students cannot assess themselves, questioning whether or not students can be trusted to do so critically. We have had teachers from kindergarten through high school make such statements until they begin to pursue self-assessment earnestly. We suspect that helping students assess themselves is one of the least developed areas of reading and writing programs. Indeed, most of the teachers that we have interviewed have very little to say when you ask them to describe how they get their students involved in learning how to assess themselves.

Student self assessment is one of the major principles undergirding the use of portfolios. Portfolios are not merely storage areas for student work. Instead, students are involved in self-assessment as they organize their portfolios, select and arrange their materials, reflect upon what they have achieved, plan their future work, share their work with others, and offer introductory critiques to accompany their work. Self-assessment is one of the major reasons for advocating the use of portfolios.

How Portfolios Support Student Self-assessment

As we reflected upon the assessment and evaluation procedures in place in most school settings, we realized that students were not involved. They were rarely even partners in the assessment and evaluation activities. Essentially it seemed as if assessment and evaluation were used to police rather than enhance learning.

Along with pursuing our goal of tying assessment to student learning and, therefore, shifting responsibility for assessment and evaluation to the students, we began to see four important prerequisites for using portfolios in self-assessment: student ownership, student-centeredness, a noncompetitive environment, and customized portfolios.

Student Ownership

Students need to be invested in the portfolio process. Students need to have a sense of ownership, which suggests that the portfolios should be viewed as the property of the student, not the teacher. The teacher may use the student portfolio to select illustrative or representative pieces of the student work, and the teacher can maintain his or her own portfolio of the student's work. But if student self-assessment is your goal, it is necessary to establish portfolios that the students consider their own. There are various ways teachers can support a feeling of ownership:

- Ensure students have a major say as to what is included or excluded;
- Maintain easy physical accessibility of the portfolios for students;
- Ask students' permission for you to share or look over their portfolio;
- Engender in classmates a respect for one another's portfolios;
- Make joint decisions on developing portfolios, sharing, and so on;
- Give students the opportunity to make choices about what they write and read.

Finally, the concept of student ownership suggests that students should be given some say in the portfolio process, including the nature of the selection process, method of self-evaluation, and sharing as well as guidelines for evaluation.

Student Centeredness

The portfolio and its appearance is secondary to involving the student in self-assessment. Unfortunately, many of us have a tendency to want to take over portfolios; that is, we may become so intent on what the end result looks like that we step in and do it for students. Some of us may not see our domineering ways as we emphasize or impose requirements pertaining to the final product that override students' involvement in the important decision-making steps of putting together, sharing, and evaluating their work. As we try to help students assess themselves, we should keep in mind:

- The portfolio process is more important than the portfolio product;
- The overriding goal is to develop self-assessment systems.

It seems key that teachers strive toward:

- Developing portfolios in partnership with students, serving as their consultant, advisor, and guide;
- Developing self-assessment systems to aid students in collecting, organizing, selecting, reflecting, and sharing;
- Understanding the student's level of competence in order to tailor comments that will broaden and support individual student thinking and growth.

Don't expect a rapid return. It may take time to develop the necessary trust with your students and time before students become connoisseurs of their efforts, improvement, and process and effective self-monitors of their progress and future goals. We have found that students' evaluations initially may seem rather glib and limited. Over time, however, they do develop in scope and depth. Their involvement in the process may be what counts more than their diagnostic skill.

Noncompetitiveness

In the primary grades at Westerville, Ohio, the teachers made what they felt was an important shift in their grading practices, which, in their view, had major ramifications for their self-assessment goals with portfolios. They shifted from grading students by comparing the students with one another to a grading system whereby students were compared with themselves. In Upper Arlington, Ohio, teachers write descriptive reports in partnership with the students to illuminate their development and achievement. In the minds of these teachers, competition between students for grades may have a detrimental effect on self-assessment. They suggest that students seemed less focused on reflecting upon their work, less willing to collaborate with others, and less likely to take ownership, make their own decisions, and so forth, when grading excluded student participation.

Customizing

We have already discussed ownership. In many ways, customizing or the tailoring of portfolios to fit particular structures is a natural outgrowth of ownership. Different students will have different contents in their portfolios, and different classrooms will have different portfolios and will pursue different portfolio process. Teachers and students should tailor the portfolios and their implementation to their situations—that is, in ways that befit their goals, their implementation of the portfolio process, and their learning experiences.

Problems arise when outsiders or institutions overly prescribe the portfolios. In our conversations with districts that have tried to introduce portfolios system-wide, a rigid preset framework for portfolios was viewed by teachers as an encumbrance rather than an enhancement. We hold the view that portfolios will not work (in the ways we would like them to) unless teachers and students initiate portfolios that fit their classrooms, students, and portfolio process. District-mandated portfolios might be viewed as off-shoots, but not the primary portfolios.

A number of proposals, which will be analyzed in the next chapter, mandate a fixed approach to the intent of portfolios and a rigid process for using portfolios. Our proposal is not intended to prescribe; instead, it takes its lead from what teachers and students develop themselves. Portfolios should be informed but not mandated by others.

Self-selection and Informal Self-assessment

"I'm not sure what to put in my portfolio. Should I include lots of different things?"

"Should I show how much I have improved?"

"These are my favorite stories. They introduce a character that I created after reading *Soup.*"

"I think that I will include my project on the survival of whales."

"I'm also going to include a section that includes my reading journal and reports. Some of my reports aren't too great. But others are stupendous."

As students mull over what they are to include, they are involved in a great deal of decision-making about what it is they value, what their work represents, what they have achieved, and how they have changed. By having to choose among various pieces, students notice differences and similarities as they discern features that would otherwise go unnoticed.

This student accomplished an enormous amount of work in one grading period. Now she faces the difficult but rewarding task of deciding how and what to select.

To what extent does this selection process prompt self-assessment? Most of the teachers who use portfolios claim that the selection process engages the students in an enormous amount of self-evaluation. Without being formalized or overly structured, students become intensely engaged in decision-making and reflecting. They use peers and the teacher as sounding boards for their decision-making. While incidental, self-assessment is both pervasive and vital.

The *self-selection* process has three aspects:

- Deciding upon the areas to be represented by the portfolios;
- Working as a class to establish procedures, criteria for self-selection, and a process for recording students' reasoning for their selections;
- Selecting representative material in these areas.

Students decide what they might include in their portfolios, with suggestions from the teacher during conferences. This can run the gamut of samples of different kinds of writing, from reports, projects, stories, songs, poems, drafts and plans to different kinds of reading responses and related material, including annotated reading lists.

The teacher and student discuss possibilities and then specify what kinds of materials will be included and how many. In one elementary classroom, the teacher and children decided to include materials related to both their reading and writing. They agreed on selecting eight examples of their work. In a high school classroom, the teachers and students agreed that they should include written reading reports from school and writing from home that represented their efforts over time.

As Sandra Murphy, who has been working with portfolios in California suggests, it seems as if teachers and children have a range of options along the following continua:

Everything	Selected Samples
Finished Products	Intermediate or Draft-level Work
Student Work	Other Information

Establishing the Criteria and Making the Selection

Once the teacher and students establish the kind and amount of material to be included, the selection procedure begins. Teachers may need to develop procedures for making selections so that students don't just rush and select with little reflection. We suggest that teachers encourage students to look over what they have done and consider the kinds of efforts that they want represented.

In one elementary classroom where students develop portfolios, they pursue a range of writing that includes:

- Stories that are their favorites;

- Reports that they thought were interesting;
- Papers that were done with others;
- Pivotal pieces;
- Companion pieces;
- Letters or messages they sent;
- Favorite journal entries;
- Papers that were their best work;
- Papers that were difficult;
- Pieces that provide a trail or "footprint" showing their development.

The students and teacher negotiate the number and kinds of material that will go into their showcase portfolio. The teacher also encourages and provides time for students to obtain comment from others about what they are planning to include. Students who have made hasty decisions on what to include usually become more reflective when a classmate makes different suggestions. Students who have difficulty making decisions tend to be spurred to make choices when others are involved.

Class discussions are effective in helping students make decisions about their work in terms of versatility, improvement, achievement, and personal relevance. By sharing student writing and reading responses over time and discussing purposes, strengths, and needs, students develop a sense of the important aspects of both writing and reading.

Students examine their portfolios periodically to decide what they have achieved and to develop future goals.

Self-evaluation Procedures

There are a host of ways more formal self-evaluation procedures can be enlisted in conjunction with the use of portfolios. These proposals tend to run the gamut from open-ended approaches to structured checklists and from student self-evaluation to peer or parent evaluation.

We should warn people about the use of many of these checklists for a number of reasons:

1. Students may not be as interested in more formal approaches to self-evaluation that require them to relay in writing what was said or could be said. Teachers have reported that students become tired of completing formal evaluations. They suggest that some students view them as just another thing they have to do.

2. The self-evaluation procedures with which teachers have reported success are those that are integrated into the students' ongoing classroom experience. For example, self evaluation comments that arise spontaneously in conversation with peers may be more meaningful and generative than the comments students offer in response to questionnaires or checklists. Students are likely to view questionnaires and checklists as ends unto themselves and less useful as resources for self-evaluation.

3. Have realistic expectations. In evaluating themselves students may appear to be saying much the same thing over and over again, and they may not say much. Over time, however, look for an expanding set of features and more definition.

4. A large number of suggestions for self-evaluation have been proposed in numerous journal and book articles that may not have been tried with children. Don't assume that the suggestions for self-evaluation have worked in classrooms. The best approach will be for you and your students to experiment with possibilities.

Some examples of more formal procedures follow:

Note cards

A number of teachers have had a great deal of success with having students use note cards to gather student self-evaluation comments for individual pieces chosen for their student portfolios. These note cards simply describe why a piece was selected for the portfolio and may include some introductory remarks stating the merits of the piece or some information about its origins. Usually teachers combine the use of note cards with having students write a brief essay describing or comparing the various elements in their portfolios.

Checklists

If you scan recent articles on assessment you will find a number of suggestions for checklists and questionnaires to guide self-assessment of a single piece of writing. While we are somewhat hesitant about using some of these because they may be untested or become ends unto themselves, we have included a compilation of some of the questions or problems that they tend to include.

A Single Piece of Writing

Name _____

Title of Piece _____

Why did you select this piece of writing?
What do you see as the strengths?
What was especially important to you when you were
    writing this piece?
What things did you wrestle with?
If you could work on this further, what would you do?
What were some of the reactions you received?
How is this the same or different from your other pieces?

A Reading Response

Why did you select your response to this story?
What did you particularly like about this selection?
How do you think others would react to this selection?
How would they agree or disagree with you?
How was this the same as or different from other things
    you have read and responded to?
How did or will this influence what you will do in the
    future?

Thinking about Yourself as a Reader or Writer

What kinds of writing (reading) have you done in the past?
What kinds of things do you like to write (read) most?
What do you like to do least?
How do you decide what you will write (read)?
What things do you spend time wrestling with as a writer/
    reader?
What are your strengths as a writer (reader)?
What have you learned to do as a writer (reader)?
What are your future goals as a writer (reader)?
How do others react to your writing (reading)?
    Looking back over your writing (reading), what do you
notice?

Thinking about Your Portfolio

What kinds of material have you included in your portfolio?
In what ways are they different? The same?
What does your portfolio reveal about you as a reader,
    writer, person?
What does your portfolio suggest your strengths are?
What does your portfolio suggest about how you have
    changed?
What do you think people will learn about you from your
    portfolio?
How do you plan to use your portfolio?

Responses by Peers and Parents

In previous chapters we described how peers and parents can offer valuable feedback and support for students' reading and writing development. This assumes that they offer meaningful support. We would hope for positive feedback. We would suggest that time be put aside to prepare peers and parents in the ways they might offer support to students. They may need guidance in being reflective listeners, supporting strengths and appreciating effort.

In a recent presentation, Roberta Camp shared a peer and teacher response form that has been used in high school classrooms.

Name _____ Period _____

Title of Paper _____

Date Written _____

Peer Evaluation I

1. What do you see as the special strength of this work?
2. What do you think was especially important to the
    writer in working on this piece?
3. Suggest one thing for the writer to focus on next in
    her/his writing.

Peer Evaluation II

1. What do you see as the special strength of this work?
2. What do you think was especially important to the
    writer in working on this piece?
3. Suggest one thing for the writer to focus on next in
    her/his writing.

Teacher Evaluation

1. What do you see as the special strength of this work?
2. What do you think was especially important to the writer in working on this piece?
3. Suggest one thing for the writer to focus on next in her/his writing.

Roberta Camp stresses that the proposed question set is exploratory and that it is important to understand how the questions are used. After students evaluate their own pieces, they use the questions in a read-around. After working through rough drafts and approaching final drafts, the students are grouped together in threes. Papers are passed around, with the questions used to initiate conversation and dialogue.

Camp sees the ensuing discussion and reflection as the essence of the portfolio process. It is important to note that this ongoing procedure is done only after the students have considered their own pieces in a similar way. Camp stresses the importance of students having a sense of ownership of their pieces prior to their being reviewed or shared with outsiders.

Additionally, teacher input occurs only after students have shared with each other. Camp mentions that students have commented that they prefer to have teacher feedback, including grading, occur after peer interaction. The students' remarks have equal legitimacy with those of the teacher since the guiding questions are the same, a point not lost on the students.

In conjunction with Roberta Camp's work in Pittsburgh Schools, Kathryn Howard (who is the middle school teacher on special assignment for Arts PROPEL Imaginative Writing), has been involved in exploring guidelines for parent review of student folders. Her forms below represent a specific and positive way of parents, and in turn, their children getting involved in the portfolio assessment process.

PARENT FOLDER REVIEW AND REFLECTION

Student _____

Reader _____

Date _____

Please read everything in your child's writing folder, including drafts and commentary. Each piece is set up in back-to-front order, from rough draft to final copy. Further, each piece is accompanied by both student and teacher comments on the piece and the writing process. Finally, the folders also include written questionnaires where students write about their strengths and weaknesses as writers.

We believe that the best assessment of student writing begins with the students themselves, but must be broadened to include the widest possible audience. We encourage you to become part of the audience.

When you have read the folders, please talk to your children about their writing. In addition, please take a few minutes to respond to these questions.

- Which piece of writing in the folders tells you most about your child's writing?

- What does it tell you?

- What do you see as the strengths in your child's writing?

- What do you see as needs to be addressed in your child's growth and development as a writer?

- What suggestions do you have which might aid the class's growth as writers?

- Other comments, suggestions?

Thank you so much for investing this time in your child's writing.

Ms. Howard

STUDENT RESPONSE TO PARENT REFLECTION

Most of you seemed to respond very positively to the experience of having your parents and/or others in your family read your writing folders.

Please take a few minutes now and respond to the following questions about your experience.

- What do you think your parents learned about you as a writer as a result of their reading your folders and discussing them with you?

- What did you learn about yourself as a writer as a result of your discussion with your parents?

- What surprised you most about the discussion?

- What suggestions do you have that might improve your discussion with your parents about your writing?

Conferences and Summits

In the portfolio classroom, "author's chair" becomes an opportunity for students to present and receive reactions to their pieces.

Conferences may be among the most vital means of supporting student self-assessment. Conferences offer a unique means of supporting student self-assessment. Unlike more formal self-evaluation procedures, conferences can follow the lead of the student and offer the support or feedback necessary to prompt as well as guide reflections.

There are at least three kinds of conferences that might be enlisted in conjunction with using portfolios:
1. Planning conferences, directed at helping students pull together their portfolios, including their self-evaluative remarks;
2. Sharing conferences, involving having students share their portfolios with classmates;
3. Formative conferences, which involve joint assessment of the portfolios by the teacher and students as they develop goals for the future.

The frequency with which such conferences are held may vary, but a reasonable goal may be to plan one every semester or grading period.

Conferences should not be viewed as ends unto themselves, finales, or opportunities to upstage others. Rather, conferences are largely intended to help students better understand their strengths and needs. To maximize such benefits from these various conferences, some planning should occur. Before the planning conference, the teacher might give one or more mini-lessons in which he or she demonstrates with one or two students how to decide what to place in the portfolio and some of the kinds of evaluative comments that might be included. Before the sharing conference, the teacher might discuss with the student (whose work is to be shared) what she or he plans to share and sample.

Some guidelines for conferencing might be established with the class. For instance, this might include developing a class list of do's and don'ts, such as the following:

Do's	Dont's
• Give the writer feedback on what you like about the selection;	• Criticize the selection;
• Comment on things that are the same and different.	• Be negative;
• Ask: Why certain pieces were chosen; What the writer learned about him/herself; What the writer plans to do next;	• Interrogate.
• Encourage comparisons and contrasts with other strategies;	
• Let the writer do most of the talking;	
• Have the writer discuss areas of improvement;	
• Enjoy the fact that different people will like different things.	

Before the summit, have the students look back over their portfolios. At this time, they might be encouraged to include some of the comments that their classmates or the teacher offered. In fact, they might include on their self-evaluations a place to quote others. In addition, they might be encouraged to complete a self-evaluation form or report directed at the portfolio as a whole. For example, they might simply respond to the following questions:

1. What can you do now that you could not do before?
2. What are some of the things that you can do very well?
3. What do you want to do next?
4. What do you want to learn next?

Logs and Journals

Logs and journals may be used to keep track of the amount of reading and writing pursued as well as reflect on ongoing achievements and future goals.

The role of logs and journals should not be minimized in supporting student self-assessment. Many teachers are familiar with reading and writing logs in which students keep track of what they have read and written. These often serve a valuable role in helping students reflect upon what they have read and written as well as their progress so far.

Less commonplace may be the use of learning logs. Learning logs are lists that students periodically develop to detail what they have accomplished and future goals. For example, in Westerville, some of the teachers have students look through their portfolios for purposes of logging their accomplishments and goals.

What I Have Learned	My Future Goals

The students will pull out their portfolios, review their work, and jot down rather expansive lists of achievements and future goals. Perhaps their analyses may lack sophistication; nonetheless, they are generally on target and thoughtful.

Journals are another invaluable means by which students can be engaged in meaningful reflection on their work and accomplishments. Journals are private places where students can record for themselves and the teacher their day-to-day experiences. How might they be used with portfolios? Some teachers encourage students to include their entire journals as part of the portfolio or to copy sections from it. Other teachers may encourage the students to refer to their journals especially the self-evaluative comments, when pulling together their portfolios, or to refer to their portfolios in their journals.

Other Approaches

The questionnaires presented here do not exhaust the possibilities. Other approaches to formalizing self-assessment are available. In some of the classrooms that we have visited, teachers have involved students in helping define the criteria for grading their work and, in turn, evaluating themselves in accordance with this criteria. Some of these practices are discussed in the next chapter. In one high school classroom, the teacher had students choose from a menu of possible criteria a subset of characteristics for which they gave themselves grades; they suggested different weights in determining an overall grade. Regie Routman, in an excellent discussion of assessment (in her update of her book *Transitions*), describes students' use of self-generated report cards. These self-generated report cards are reports that students prepare on themselves.

Analysis of Student Self-assessment

A study conducted by one of the authors focuses on analyzing students' self-assessments of material included in portfolios. Preliminary findings indicate that students' self-assessments mature over time. Specifically, students' comments change in the following ways:
1. Number of comments increase;
2. Comments focus on more aspects of writing;
3. Comments become more focused on both personal and community expectations;
4. Students begin to notice growth through comparisons with previous work;
5. Students' ability to evaluate their total performance increases.

Over the course of a one-year period, students produced successively more comments about their work during each grading period. As portfolios grew to encompass both recent and past pieces, students had more opportunities to evaluate their work, which increases student reliability.

As the number of comments increases, so does the breadth of the comments. Students evaluate from personal views of what is important, and their evaluations exceed the traditional focuses of usage, style, handwriting, and form. When students are given an opportunity to evaluate writing that is important to them, they consider purpose, topic, personal relevance of the piece and personal qualities (effort, feelings) as well as other aspects.

Student assessments begin to be systematic. Students monitor their progress toward accomplishing their goals as well as goals or criteria that the classroom community of students has discussed. During the course of the year, students begin to use previous pieces to show areas of specific improvement. They become acutely aware of all of their work and are able to notice small improvements from piece to piece.

As student involvement and awareness of their own work

grew, students grew in their ability to make decisions about their overall portfolio contents. In other words, pieces are put into portfolios for expanding purposes: to show new achievements, to illustrate versatility, and to show personal interests. Over time students began to notice the ways in which all of the elements in their portfolio form a composite picture of themselves.

A Final Word and Warning

Perhaps because of the newness of the topic of self-evaluation, we wish to close with an expression of concern. As we have worked with teachers on developing self-evaluation systems, especially formal approaches such as questionnaires, notecards, and logs, we have noticed a couple of problematic tendencies. First, making students overly conscious of what they are learning and achieving has the potential to interfere with the spontaneous excitement of writing. It would be a horrible world if all of our experiences demanded analysis. Second, we worry about the criteria that may be enlisted by students to make evaluative analysis. In some classrooms, criteria may emerge that misdirects students to low-level conventions (e.g. spelling and punctuation) rather than get at the heart or the essence of a specific selection. Furthermore, the same criteria may be applied to different works and so on. We would hate to see self-evaluation become wall charts suggesting fixed criteria by which students assess themselves.

Portfolios Available Through Publishing Houses

Several school text publishers and test development houses are producing portfolios. They include:
- The Riverside Integrated Literature and Language Arts Portfolio
- Psychological Corporation, Integrated Language Arts Portfolio
- Silver-Burdett and Ginn
- D.C. Heath
- Harcourt, Brace, and Jovanovich
- Scott Foresman and Company

While we laud the direction of such efforts, at the same time we also caution consumers. Portfolios should be viewed as vehicles for student self-evaluation and assessment practices rooted in the life of the classroom and the world of the student. Sometimes prepackaged portfolios may work against the customization, flexibility, and differential use of portfolios by teachers and students. We recommend that such attempts be subjected to the analysis described in the chapter "A Survey of Portfolio Projects."

Chapter 8

Portfolio Analysis
and
Record Keeping

Portfolios increase the visibility of students. When wide collections of reading and writing can be viewed over an extended period of time, teachers are able to see patterns of strengths and needs. One of the strengths of portfolios is the teacher interventions they make possible. To take full advantage of information gleaned from portfolios, many teachers keep anecdotal records from conferences, make analytic notes while viewing portfolios, and consolidate intervention possibilities on different checklists.

Anecdotal Records from Portfolio Conferences

In one fifth grade classroom the teacher holds a variety of conferences with his students. The teacher has many informal daily conferences, but in the heat of classroom life it is impractical to record everything from these brief sessions. The teacher therefore holds monthly portfolio conferences with each student. During the scheduled conferences the teacher jots down notes in a record book. Anecdotal notes from monthly reading and writing portfolio conferences are shown below. The students bring their portfolio, their current writing projects, and books they are reading to the conference.

This teacher views the teacher-student assessment conference as a time to engage with students in a partnership that celebrates achievement and provides direction for the future through setting goals.

In the conference the teacher and student meet face to face. Comments are focused on specific aspects of a student's writing or reading. This ensures communication on points that are specific to the student's needs. The teacher keeps records of current reading or writing, notes whether student entries are up to date in their journals, notes strengths and needs, and provides instructional suggestions during the session.

The information this teacher learns during the portfolio conference is used to focus instruction during daily brief encounters, to develop end of term reports, as well as to form short-term small groups for instruction on topics with which several students need help.

Notes for Portfolio Analysis

At the end of each grading period, this teacher reviews each portfolio in-depth. Three broad categories along with a menu of possible areas for comment are used to help the teacher focus analytic comments. The teacher notes overall characteristics, reading strengths and needs, and writing strengths and needs. The analysis form below illustrates notes taken during the full portfolio analysis of one fifth-grade student's portfolio.

Obviously the teacher's anecdotal records are for his personal use. The comments he has written about the portfolio reveal qualitative features that can be focused on during instructional contacts as well as shared with parents during confer-

Portfolio Writing Conference

Name of Student: *Chris*

Observations:

Date	Topic	Form	Mechanical Skills	Strengths	Needs	Suggestions	Problem Solving	Self-Analysis	On-going Goals	Resource/ Sharing
11/23	camping story	fiction	good	Descriptive eq. Strong voice.	"Tell." No dialogue	Try to use dialogue			Revise w/ dialogue	Discussed story line w/ peers.
1/13	Maya's Party	pers. narr.		detail			Had many ideas!	Focused on handwriting		
1/30	?		Didn't have a topic. Brainstormed—decided on trip to convince.							
2/15	Convince House			Has written many pieces!	but it went several places incomp.	Focus on one piece.	Discussed time frame		Finish convince house.	
3/20	The Zoo	poem	Spelling good. good structure	Imagery descriptive words.				word choice good. Flees! Fun poem.	Write more poetry	

Portfolio Reading Conference

Name of Student: Karen

Observations:

Date	Current Books/Literature Journal	Finished	Reading	Strengths	Needs	Suggestions	Problem Solving	Self-Analysis	On-going Goals	Resource/Sharing
9/14	Sara Bishop	10/5	Fluent. Self-corrects (embellishing-details)	Reads easily			Self-corrects, pay's attn to story logic!	Feels she reads slowly.	Read more books.	Made book choice after consulting w/ peers.
11/7	Soldier's Secret	12/5		Reads consistently, widely	wants articles/event/effect meaning	Tape her reading				
11/28	Witch of B.B. Pond		Miscues (simplify, stiffen)	Good ranging! story line. Personal evaluation of book.		Discussed		Likes to read, esp. fiction	Reading book for Ocean project.	

Portfolio Analysis

Name: Molly
Date: Fall

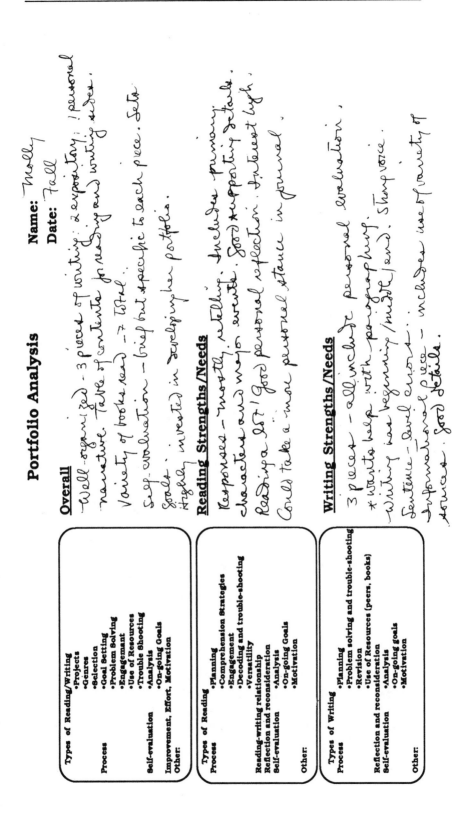

Overall

Well-organized - 3 pieces of writing: 2 expository; 1 personal narrative. Table of contents for reading and writing titles. Variety of books read → listed. Self-evaluation - brief but specific to each piece. Sets goals. Invested in developing her portfolio. High.

Reading Strengths/Needs

Responses - mostly retelling. Includes primary characters and major events. Good supporting details. Readings 26? Good personal reflection. Interest high. Could take a more personal stance in journal.

Writing Strengths/Needs

3 pieces - all include personal evaluation. + Wants help with paragraphing. Writing has beginning/middle/end. Strong voice. Sentence- and word errors. Informational piece - includes use of variety of sources. Good details.

Types of Reading/Writing
- Projects
- Genres
- Selection

Process
- Goal Setting
- Problem Solving
- Engagement
- Use of Resources
- Trouble Shooting

Self-evaluation
- Analysis
- On-going Goals

Improvement, Effort, Motivation
Other:

Types of Reading
Process
- Planning
- Comprehension Strategies
- Engagement
- Decoding and trouble-shooting
- Versatility

Reading-writing relationship
Reflection and reconsideration
Self-evaluation
- Analysis
- On-going Goals
- Motivation

Other:

Types of Writing
Process
- Planning
- Problem solving and trouble-shooting
- Revision
- Use of Resources (peers, books)

Reflection and reconsideration
Self-evaluation
- Analysis
- On-going goals
- Motivation

Other:

ences. Furthermore, the teacher has noted student self-evaluations. This student has accurately recorded her confusion with correct paragraphing in a self-evaluative comment. The teacher noted the student's desire in this area and followed through with a mini-lession to meet this need. Collaboration like this helps the teacher to develop instructional focuses that honor the students' readiness and reveals to students that they are heard and respected as full members in a classroom that addresses their concerns.

Checklists

Often there is a need to compile information in a form that affords a composite picture of the entire class so students' needs can be addressed efficiently through short term small group mini-lessons.

There are a host of ways teachers can manage and store on-going student files, while keeping them accessible to students.

Vehicles for "on-the-run" assessment are integral to successful record-keeping and management. Teachers can make forms suited to their own classroom needs.

In the sample checklist above, the teacher notes characteristics from conferences and from a portfolio analysis. The teacher uses a simple checking system where a + illustrates strong performance, illustrates adequate progress, and a — denotes a need for instructional emphasis.

Portfolio Criteria

Name	#	Self Eval.	Versatility	Response	Surface Features	Text Features	Problem Solving	Improvement	Motivation
Jenny	✓+	✓	✓	– reTelling	– hand writing	– ot lack of develop.	✓	✓	✓
Sue	✓+	✓+	✓+	✓	✓	✓	✓+	✓	✓+
Linda	✓+	✓	✓	–	– revision	✓	–	✓	✓
Harold	✓+	✓	✓	–	✓	– lack of depth	–	✓+	✓+
Lynn	✓	– not detailed	– form	–	✓	– listing	–	✓	✓
Steven	✓	✓+	– (both new)	✓	– hand writing	✓	✓	✓	✓

The teacher may use the checklist to form short term mini-lesson groups or other support. By glancing down categories the teacher can see who would benefit from similar specific lessons, small group conferences, networking between students, or the provision of resources.

Portfolio Analysis Guide

In this classroom criteria for portfolios are decided upon by the entire class. A holistic analysis guide was developed based on levels of performance on the criteria. This guide can be used to analyze portfolios by comparing each portfolio with descriptors in each category. This type of guide should be developed and understood by participating students. The primary intent is not to rank order students but to focus attention on descriptors to illuminate possible areas for interventions to extend or support for the student's individual growth. The guide is intended for analysis of individual work rather than as a comparative analysis across a group of students.

Descriptors that focus teacher attention can be noted during portfolio analysis and can serve as another source of information for communication about students' present level of performance.

Continua of Descriptors

A series of continua can also be used to plot individual students' achievements. An example of one such continua is shown below. By plotting student performance several times during the school year, student growth becomes more visible.

Portfolio Analysis Guide

Beginning

Students may appear to be at beginning stages for a number of different reasons: they may be emerging learners or learners who are only partially engaged with the classroom community in this activity. They have yet to realize their full potential; they may not be aware of or engage with their potential. These portfolios exhibit:

- Some or very little versatility, little risk-taking in trying out new forms, a preference for routine tasks over exploration.
- Detachment from the portfolio process.
- Unidimensional self-evaluations: either global statements or focusing on one aspect of the work.
- Individual pieces reflect inexperience with written organization, standard English conventions, and/or written development of ideas. Their message may be distorted due to surface-feature errors.
- Responses include brief restatement of an incident and little evidence of personal stance or involvement.
- Limited interest in or use of reading and writing beyond classroom requirements.
- On-going goals and goal-setting processes are either global or sketchy.
- Improvement: few shifts apparent.
- Problem-solving processes reflect few resources, disengagement, lack of confidence, and/or lack of motivation.
- Limited use of resources such as sharing or peer input.

Intermediate

Developing learner exhibits strengths and independence in selected areas and potential yet to be realized in others. These portfolios exhibit:

- Expanding versatility.
- A reasonable effort to complete the portfolio with some attention to detail, organization, and overall aesthetics.
- Self-evaluations which may be multidimensional but lack specific details and/or breadth.
- Individual pieces that falter on more than one feature. For example, papers may meander from the topic at times or there may be significant spelling or punctuation errors. The pieces in the portfolio falter in development, structure, and/or sophistication of ideas without distorting the central message.
- Responses include comments about important incidents, but their focus is narrow and has little development.
- Some interest in using reading and writing beyond assignments in classroom.
- Goal setting occurs, but is restricted or does not grow or shift across time.
- Depends on repetitive use of strategies for problem-solving.
- May use resources and support in a rote fashion.

Advanced

More fully engaged, independent learner. These portfolios exhibit:

- Versatility in the variety of forms chosen.
- Clear organization of contents.
- Multidimensional self-evaluations that include reflections about a wide variety of observed traits: process, text features, surface features, voice, word choice, audience awareness, perspective, and purpose.
- Individual pieces which: have a strong voice, stay on topic, are well-organized, have well-formed sentences, and demonstrate effective word choice.
- Reponses represent strong engagement and understanding of story elements; key issues are discussed.
- Uses reading and writing for many different reasons. Motivated to go beyond class as signments.
- Goal-setting is expansive and shifts in relevant ways across time.
- Problem-solving involves using various resources in expansive and meaningful ways.
- Flexible use of resources and support.

Continua of Descriptors

Strong Performance   Needs Improvement

Versatility

Wide variety of reading and writing across genre.	Some variety	Little or no variety. Collection shows little breadth or depth.

Process

Samples reveal discoveries or pivotal learning experiences.	Process illustrated in inflexible or mechanistic ways.	Minimal use of process to reflect on achievements.

Response

Engaged with story Discusses key issues Evidence of critical questioning.	Personal reflection but focus is narrow.	Brief retelling of isolated events.

Self-Evaluations

Multidimensional Wide variety of observations.	Developing insights Some specifics noted	Single focus, global in nature.
Establishing meaningful goals.	Limited goal setting.	Goal setting too broad or non-existent.
Notes improvement.	Vague idea of improvement.	

Individual Pieces

Strong control of a variety of elements: organization, cohesion, surface features, etc.	Growing command evidenced. Some flaws but major ideas are clear.	Needs to improve: sophistication of ideas, text features, and surface features.

Problem Solving

Wrestles with problems using various resources. Enjoys problem solving and learning new ways.	Uses limited resources. Wants quick fix.	Seems helpless. Frustrated by problems.

Purposefulness/Uses

Uses reading & writing to satisfy various goals including sharing with others.	Uses reading & writing to meet others' goals.	Apathetic, resistant.

Clearly the intent of any continuum or scoring guide should be to focus teachers and students on strengths, needs, improvements, efforts, and growth from collaborative reflection. Setting criteria for portfolio assessment should be pursued cautiously and with student input. Criteria will vary as students become more sophisticated readers and writers, and should reflect their new understandings. It has been our experience that student self-evaluations should not be limited by a narrow list of traits. When given an opportunity to reflect openly on their work students' comments are refreshingly honest and insightful. Many times their reasons for including a piece in a portfolio is because it has high personal significance. Remembering that the portfolio is first and foremost a student-owned collection of most highly-prized work should help us to proceed cautiously— because of the possibility of offending a child by telling him or her that their best work is unsatisfactory.

Anecdotal records, checklists, continua, and scoring guides facilitate an understanding of students' strengths and needs. The intent is to build, over time, a complete record that reveals achievements, needs, effort, growth, and reflection about accomplishments. Through these records the teacher and student can better understand the breadth and depth of student work, and together with the student, can form goals for future work.

Analyzing A Portfolio

One fifth grader in his autumn writing portfolio included three samples of his writing: a poem about the wind, an article about Olympic boxing, and an informational piece about high jumping:

Over the past 88 the high Jump sk improved 31.4% height has increa inches or 1 foot The United states has Dominated this Sport by winning the gold 12 of 20 times and the first Seven in a row. The gold medel has only excaped 8 times by six Differnt countries E. Germany and W.Germany bouth won it once, poland, canada and Australia all wan it once and the USSR won 3 times.

High Jump   Sept. 8

In this piece of writing I like the information but its is flat in cursive and its not to long but the informaton is great I like the percentage.

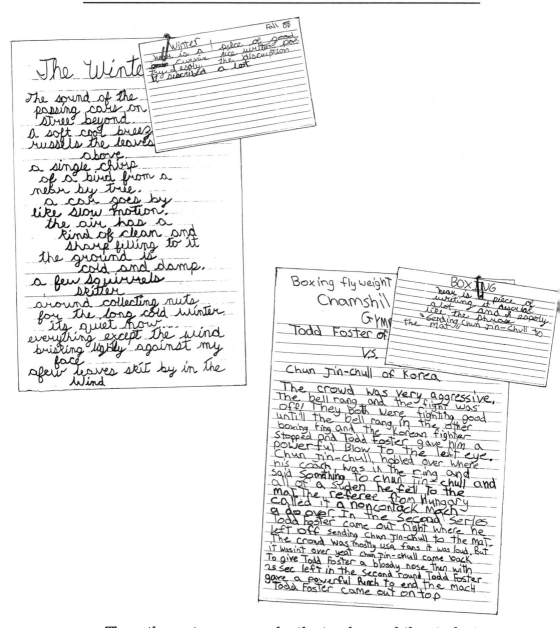

These three pieces are works the teacher and the student discussed in writing conferences while the pieces were in progress and are only a small portion of the student's total writing collection. The three pieces this student chose for his showcase portfolio represent his perceptions of his best work during September, October, and November.

This fifth grade student writes in three different forms. He is able to express himself clearly and is willing to take risks with language and form. He sustains a topic and communicates his message clearly to an audience. Each piece has been revised.

This student finds writing tedious but is willing to persist until he has reached a final product. These pieces represent a lot of work for the student at this point in the school year. The comments he has written about each piece reflect only some of his thoughts about his work. Such comments can emanate from a conference or from sharing. On the surface, they reveal that he is concerned and aware of his use of language. He says about his boxing piece: "I especially like the phrase, 'sending Chun Jin-Chull to the mat.'"

He comments on the use of "good" cursive writings in his poem and points out that he has "described a lot." He also distinguishes between forms of writing. He attends to the informational piece by commenting on his use of information and especially his use of percentages.

We see the teacher's function as helping the students reflect upon their work. To that end, the teacher might view conferences as a time to encourage further reflection by asking the child:

- What other things did you like?
- What things did you wrestle with?
- Were there things you discovered as you wrestled with this _____?
- How is this like other things you have done or planned to do?

At the same time the teacher might share with the student his or her thoughts as well as comments others might make. For example, the teacher might talk about the events described by the student or other stories, poems, and so forth, of which the teacher was reminded. The teacher could comment on the richness and power of the language. Most importantly, the teacher could have the student reflect on what might happen to the text (sharing, publishing, etc.) and future goals. Finally, the teacher might jot down some notes detailing the student's interests and comments pertaining to strategies and skills.

This particular student's teacher chose aspects of his work to focus on and praise. His teacher, for example, noted that the student approaches planning by enlisting input from peers and revises with a great deal of (maybe too much) concern for neatness. His work demonstrates a growing awareness of audience by providing the information an outsider would need to know to understand the circumstances, and it shows the author's poem is rich with imagery. He clearly is working on a form that works for this free verse poem and he is successful at capturing the growing sense of winter's presence. Furthermore, he enjoys mulling over what should be selected to go into his portfolio and has two or three comments about his work. All of these characteristics should be celebrated with this writer.

Based upon the conference, the teacher might offer some suggestions for proceeding. The teacher might note that over time this student could benefit from having a facilitator help him extend his ideas; each piece is short and could be enriched with additional information. The student might be given some help with revision, a process the teacher feels the writer has little patience for at this time. This type of assistance would help the student develop new ideas, although feedback of this sort would have to be done carefully to avoid frustrating a budding writer. The student could also benefit from some instruction about paragraphing as well as drawing his attention to other minor mechanical and spelling errors that may help tighten his editing skills. The student himself should be asked what his goals are for improving his writing.

Certainly, there are many strengths and needs this writer exhibits in his portfolio. A look at this student's subsequent portfolio would reveal his growth in the areas the teacher and student chose to discuss.

Parental Review, Feedback, and Reflection

Often we encounter experiences that turn our stomachs about assessment and parental involvement. These stories range from parents becoming disillusioned with their child's abilities to young adolescents becoming sufficiently depressed about their performance and the reaction of family members to their reported progress that they drop out or even contemplate or commit suicide. We need to begin to ask ourselves how can we re-orient assessment so that our students, parents and the school are working together in positive and productive ways.

How might we approach parental involvement? As procedures and criteria are developed for analyzing portfolios, parents should be involved and considered as an audience for and contributor to both the students' portfolios and methods for reporting student progress. We would like to see parents engaged in offering input about their children Furthermore, as methods are developed for reporting student progress using information available in the students' portfolio, we hope that parents are involved in offering input and, in turn, that they will understand the information that is reported. The school-based assessment plan should nourish a positive ongoing relationship between the child, the parent and the school.

We would suggest that you begin with informational meetings, open houses, memos outlining the nature of assessment practices as well as conferences with parents individually. Unless parents are informed in face to face meetings, by telephone or with clearly presented background information on carefully crafted portfolio-based reports or analysis schemes, they may not understand the information they are sent or they may interpret the reported progress of their child negatively. We should ask ourselves: How we might develop a parent's understanding? How might we obtain input from the parents? How might we develop a reciprocal relationship with the parent that works for the child?

We try to use the following guidelines when we conference with the child's parents:

1. Give the parent advance notice that you will be contacting them about setting up a conference;

2. Invite the parents either by phone, face to face, or in conjunction with preestablished parental evenings;

3. Have on hand the student's portfolio and other relevant information such as his or her ongoing folder. In several of the school districts there exists ongoing literacy folders or profiles which are part of the student's permanent file.

4. Create a situation that is comfortable, non-threatening, and that allows you to work collaboratively with the parent. Sit side-by side rather than across from one another. If the parent's language is other than your own, prearrange for an interpreter.

5. Keep the focus on having a conversation about the child. Some of the areas that you might discuss are: the types of stories and reports that the child likes reading and writing; particular interests of the child that might be drawn upon; how the child spends her or his time outside of school and the types of interactions he or she has with siblings and parents; changes that the parents and you have observed; opportunities that the parents might pursue at home; opportunities that the parents would like for their child; and so on.

6. Ask open-ended questions, ask parents to expand upon points, ask them to provide illustrations, as you talk about the child's progress refer to the portfolio and related forms upon which you have been keeping tabs on their child.

7. Pull together the conference in some form of collaborative summary for both yourself and the parent to keep. Write up summary as part of your ongoing literacy folder for the child. In future conferences, you can refer back to the summary.

*As an aside, the format we have outlined for a parent confer-
ence parallels the types of negotiations that we would like to see
occur between the child and the teacher periodically.*

Report cards serve a major role in informing parents about
their child's progress. Unfortunately, we suspect that they create
more problems than they solve. Oftentimes, the report cards'
forms themselves reflect a very narrow view of the student's
reading and writing. The comments or grades tend to represent
a form of summarization that fails to do justice to the child's
reading and writing experiences—their diversity, his improvements, her efforts, ongoing learning goals and so on. Examinations of the think-alouds of teachers as they determine grades
suggest that decisions tend to be forced to fit the grade or made
using criteria which seems objective but may in actuality be
arbitrary. Moreover, most report cards tend to compare students
with A's, B's, C's, or D's or categories that can be easily translated
to mean the same kinds of evaluations of success or failure which
work against the view of the child as an ongoing learner.

As we have contemplated the use of report cards in conjunction with portfolios, we encourage teachers to consider the
following guidelines:

1. Keep the report cards as open-ended as possible
2. Focus on the student's achievements and ongoing learning goals rather than weaknesses
3. Expand the menu of possible topics for discussion on the
   report cards to include those which follow from portfolio
   use (see analysis forms)
4. Involve the students in pursuing a collaborative report

Permanent School-based Portfolios: Meeting the Needs of Next Year's Teacher and other Stakeholders

Frequently we are asked by administrators and teachers Can
the student portfolio becomes part of the school's permanent
record? Can some kind of score or analysis of the portfolio serve
in its place? Our response tends to be "Yes and No."

Yes, we like the idea of the school maintaining an ongoing
portfolio of the students' reading and writing and other activities
such as science, art, and so forth, which is updated by the
teacher in collaboration with the students on an annual or semi-
annual basis. This should not replace the student's own portfolio
which he or she maintains and retains. There should be two
portfolios: the student's own portfolio and a portfolio that is part
of the child's ongoing permanent folder. Certainly, they may
share some things in common and relate to one another, but we
see them as serving somewhat distinct audiences and purposes.
Whereas the student's portfolio is a vehicle largely for student
reflection, teacher reflection and parents, the ongoing school-
based portfolio can serve as a vehicle for resource teachers, next

year's teacher, administrators and other stake-holders. While the student's portfolio is intended to capture the student's work and reflections related to the particular kinds of experiences that emerge from particular classrooms, the school-based portfolio may be more structured and call for certain kinds of inclusions from different classrooms. The student's portfolio can serve as the basis for selecting material for the school-based portfolio, but should not displace or replace it. Furthermore, it should not be detached from the student.

An interesting proposal along these lines is currently being developed by Bay Village, Ohio. The superintendant at Bay Village has proposed that an ongoing permanent portfolio be part of the permanent records for all of the district's students. Upon graduation the student would receive his or her portfolio along with his or her diploma.

We do support the use and incorporation of various portfolio analysis forms and procedures. However, it is key to use analysis procedures that reflect the nature of portfolios and their potential rather than some preset notions, yardsticks, or motivations that limit the possibilities or work in opposition to the possibilities with portfolios. Among the methods proposed to analyze portfolio that we have reviewed in the next chapter are some which approach portfolio analysis in a rigid versus flexible, unidimensional rather than multi-dimensional, as well as detached rather than collaborative fashion. We view such proposals as problematic. In other words, we support proposal for analyzing portfolios in terms of features that reflect the nature of portfolios rather than those that do not.

In the current chapter we have tried to describe what we see as some possibilities. The following flowchart represents an overview of how we envision the portfolio process. We would hope that our proposal is more suggestive than prescriptive.

Collaborative Portfolio Development, Refinement,

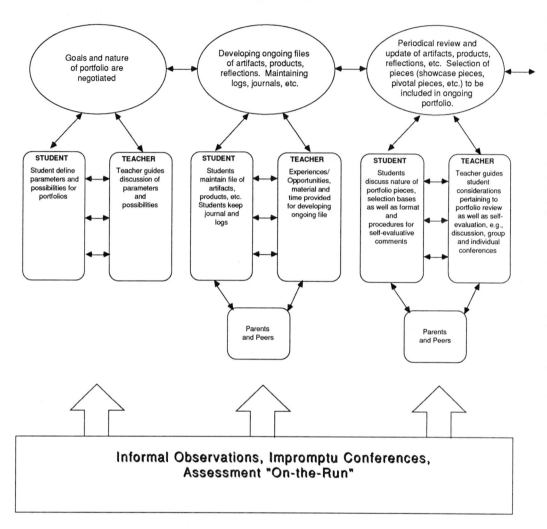

Reflection, Analysis, and Reporting

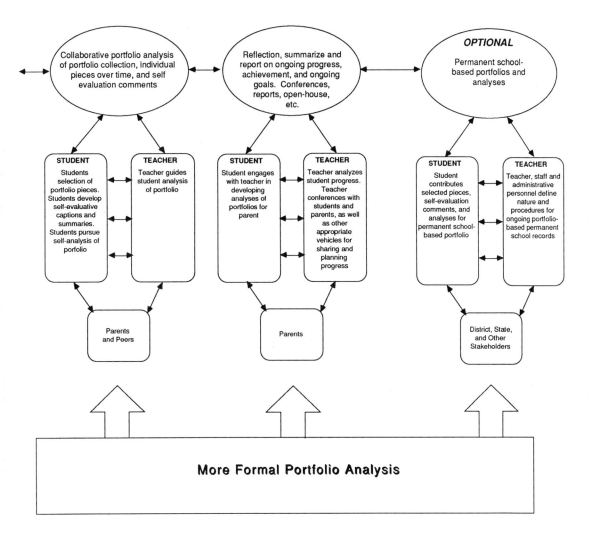

Part Three

Portfolios in Context

Chapter 9

A Survey of Portfolios

At a recent meeting, a colleague made the comment that portfolios were worthwhile but would not survive long in schools "since you can't score or grade them, and whether or not you like it, society demands scores." We both agree and disagree with him. We agree that it is unfortunate that society demands scores. We would add that it seems unfortunate that schools might try to score or grade portfolios. But we disagree that it can't be done. In fact, a number of proposals exist for doing so.

This chapter attempts to describe some of the proposals that have evolved. Before describing these efforts, we would like to emphasize the following points:

1. We would prefer that portfolios were not scored or graded but that students' efforts be evaluated through descriptions that illustrate individual strengths and needs;

2. If they are graded, we would like to see multiple grades differentiating a variety of aspects of student achievement, effort, and goals. Ideally, we prefer narrative comments that capture the individual and what he or she has done and is doing.

This should come as no surprise since it seems almost hypocritical to pursue simplification, standardization, and objectivity when portfolios are based upon notions of complexity, individuality, and subjectivity.

Overview of Selected Evaluation Schemes

The state of Vermont, the Educational Testing Service, selected university groups, various school districts, and classroom teachers have drafted proposals for using portfolios as a basis for evaluating individuals. In general, there seems to be a number of dimensions that characterize the variations that are being proposed. The following tables depict the variations that we see across the purposes for using portfolios, their use as sources of data for making judgments, the criteria applied to the data sources, the involvement of participants, and the kind of summary developed.

Each proposal will be reviewed across the dimensions outlined on the Proposal Characteristics, and the summary chart below will be used to synopsize the characteristics of each proposal. The dimensions are defined in the summary chart on p. 149.

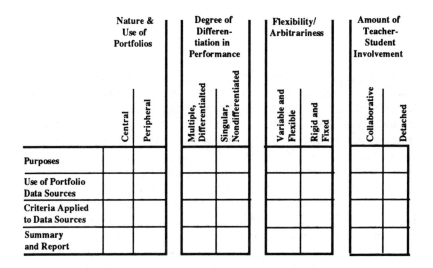

	Nature & Use of Portfolios		Degree of Differentiation in Performance		Flexibility/ Arbitrariness		Amount of Teacher-Student Involvement	
	Central	Peripheral	Multiple, Differentialted	Singular, Nondifferentiated	Variable and Flexible	Rigid and Fixed	Collaborative	Detached
Purposes								
Use of Portfolio Data Sources								
Criteria Applied to Data Sources								
Summary and Report								

Examples of Using Portfolios to Evaluate Students

A High School Classroom

Background

Prior to using portfolios, a high school English teacher had students submit new work to her for grading. Her method of grading was tied to a computation of scores she gave to various aspects of their work or assignment. For example, with essays they had written on two books they had read, points were awarded for evidence of development and planning, first draft, use of peer input, and final draft.

The teacher set her criteria and awarded the final grade.

	Central	vs.	Peripheral	Multiple & Differential	vs.	Singular & Restricted	Variable & Flexible	vs.	Rigid & Fixed	Collaborative	vs.	Detached
Purposes	Portfolios serve as the major source for assessment data.		Portfolios are used to substantiate or complement other data such as standardized tests.	Purposes may include: overall achievement, improvement, process, range of abilities & activities, criterion-based.		Purposes restricted to assessment of overall proficiency.	Purposes may vary from portfolio to portfolio, individual to individual, site to site.		Purposes for evaluating portfolio tend to be predetermined.	Evaluation involves students, parents, & teachers negotiating purposes for evaluating portfolios.		Evaluation purposes are developed without ongoing negotiation between involved partners.
Sources of Data	Portfolio material is the basis for making judgments.		Portfolio material is compared with and does not displace other data sources such as test scores.	Various features of portfolios are examined in terms of repertoire of multiple abilities. Range, improvement, and other aspects may be considered.		Single samples, such as representative writing sample are selected as basis for evaluation.	Portfolios are delved into for possibilities that serve as evidence for a range of abilities or for suggesting patterns.		Method of selecting samples is predetermined and standardized.	Teachers and students collaborate with others on the data sources that are selected as part of the evaluation.		The data sources are defined in such a way that minimal teacher or student contact is needed.
Criteria	Criteria reflect the kinds of information that portfolios avail; criteria tied to the students' actual literacy experiences.		Criteria applied to portfolios may not represent the essential features of the portfolio.	Multiple criteria are developed while examining various aspects of portfolios. Criteria yield a wide variety of descriptive terms and are not viewed as the sole standards.		A single criteria is imposed upon the portfolio material or a subset of these materials.	Criteria may vary from portfolio to portfolio as features emerge.		A fixed criteria is applied in the same way across different portfolios.	Criteria are developed in cooperation with students and are informed by their comments.		Criteria are developed without input from teachers and students.
Summary and Report	Porfolios serve as a primary source in developing narrative description of reporting a listing of features.		Portfolios are used as additional or optional information to existing reports.	Provides differential and descriptive detail as a variety of aspects of the portfolios.		Tends to be restricted to a single summary-like scale.	Differential & descriptive information is apt to vary in accordance with differences across students & their portfolios.		Tends to place portfolio assessment on a single scale that assumes comparability and standization across portfolios.	Teachers, students, & others collaborate on the formation of summary reports.		Outsiders develop summary reports.

Figure 9.1: Summary Chart

The teacher then decided to use the portfolio as the major basis for evaluating students. She engaged students in helping her to develop guidelines for the features included in the portfolios, to identify possible criteria that might apply to select material for the portfolios, and to corroborate with her both in awarding points for various aspects of their portfolio and in determining the overall final grade.

Purpose

- To evaluate the student's portfolio;
- To engage students in collaborative self-assessment;
- To determine a final grade for course performance.

Process

At the end of the course, the students developed showcase portfolios from work they completed during the course. The students and the teacher identified the general guidelines for the portfolio; and the criteria that might apply for grading their own portfolio (with peer input), and they shared portfolios with classmates. After sharing portfolios, students offered each other feedback and used the criteria as a basis for evaluating their portfolios prior to submitting them to the teacher for her evaluation.

Evaluation Process

Goals of portfolios are discussed and negotiated with students.

↓

Guidelines and procedures for developing showcase are determined, as well as sources of material and criteria.

↓

Showcase portfolio is developed by student with peer input.

↓

Self-evaluation comments are developed and showcase portfolios presented.

↓

Students select criteria to apply to portfolio and evaluate the portfolio in these terms.

↓

Portfolio is submitted to teacher. Teacher reviews portfolio, student self-evaluative comments, and criteria scores and then awards grade.

↓

Portfolios are returned to students.

Sources for Evaluation

The students and the teacher discussed features they should include in the portfolio and to be used as the basis for evaluation. They set up as goals for the portfolio:
- A range of projects from school assignments and writing outside of school;
- A presentation based upon those projects as well as the folder that organizes their materials;
- Self-evaluative comments that describe the portfolio selections.

Criteria for Evaluation

The students and the teacher identified a list of criteria against which portfolios might be evaluated. Each student was responsible for selecting at least four criteria that were to be applied to the portfolio; deciding the weight or maximum number of points that these selected areas of criteria might receive; and evaluating his or her own portfolios on these terms. Students' portfolios and their evaluations were then submitted to the teacher. Possible criteria from which they selected included:
- Evidence of improvement;
- Evidence of effort;
- Quality of self-evaluation;
- Range of projects;
- Presentation;
- Future goals.

Summarizing and Reporting

The teacher returned the portfolios with a set of scores for each criterion and comments. The final grades were based on an aggregation of the subscores.

Qualitative Analysis of Portfolio Evaluation Procedure

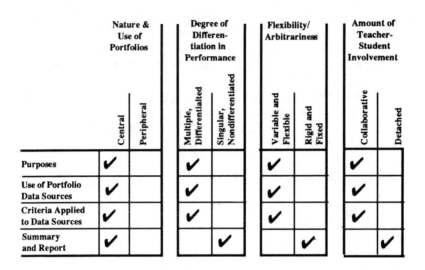

	Nature & Use of Portfolios		Degree of Differentiation in Performance		Flexibility/ Arbitrariness		Amount of Teacher-Student Involvement	
	Central	Peripheral	Multiple, Differentialted	Singular, Nondifferentiated	Variable and Flexible	Rigid and Fixed	Collaborative	Detached
Purposes	✔		✔		✔		✔	
Use of Portfolio Data Sources	✔		✔		✔		✔	
Criteria Applied to Data Sources	✔		✔		✔		✔	
Summary and Report	✔			✔		✔		✔

Comments

Portfolios contributed to a shift in this high school teacher's evaluation procedures from being teacher-controlled to collaborative. Students became more engaged in the evaluation process. Perhaps the method of summarizing could have been more descriptive, affording greater flexibility and offering more variation from student to student.

An Elementary School Classroom

Background

Prior to using portfolios, the teacher had students keep their material in folders. At the end of each quarter, he would develop, using his notes, a written narrative of each student's progress, for which he would obtain feedback from the students. When he introduced portfolios and student self-assessment, his focus shifted to having students scrutinize their own work, select representative samples of their efforts, and develop self-evaluative comments of these selected efforts and their overall performance. Instead of his writing narrative summaries based upon his notes, his end-of-quarter evaluation moved toward cultivating the students' achievements and offering feedback on their evaluations of their achievement and future goals. The teacher still developed written narratives, but this was informed by the students and characterized by greater collaboration between teacher and students.

Purposes

- To engage the students in periodical self-evaluation of their achievements, efforts and improvements;
- To help the students establish future goals;
- To confer with students on their progress and future plans;
- To develop written narrative on their work.

Process

At the end of every grading period the students sort through the reading and writing projects they have pursued. They select those that they wish to include in their portfolios, using note-cards (clipped to the various pieces) to write their reasons for selecting each piece and to explain its origin. Upon completing their reading-writing portfolio, they develop a self-evaluation summary of their portfolio detailing what they see as their strengths and future goals. These self-evaluation summaries are submitted with the portfolios to the teacher, who meets with them as he is developing his written narratives. The teacher plans interventions that guide future contacts with individual and small groups.

Evaluation Process

The teacher and students discuss the goals of portfolio, the nature of the process, possible guidelines for selecting materials, and features that might be mentioned in the self-evaluation report.

↓

Students collect reading and writing work.

↓

Students select reading and writing pieces to be included in portfolios and consult with peers, parents, and teachers. They develop self-evaluation notecards for each piece.

↓

Students review entire portfolio and develop a self-evaluative summary.

↓

Portfolio, self-evaluation cards, and summary are shared with teacher and parents.

↓

Teacher holds a conference with each student.

Sources for Evaluation

The class agrees to limit each student to a certain number of pieces: in this case, eight. Sources for pieces include projects, reports, stories, letters, journal entries, reader-response sheets, and so forth.

Criteria for Evaluation

The students and teacher discuss possible criteria that might guide students' choices but they do not set any fixed criteria and self-evaluation. Students are encouraged to make selections and to develop self-evaluative statements with comments from peers.

Summarizing and Reporting

Each student's self-evaluation note cards and summary serves as the basis for a conference with the teacher, which, in turn, frames the teacher's narrative summary.

Qualitative Analysis of Portfolio Evaluation Procedure

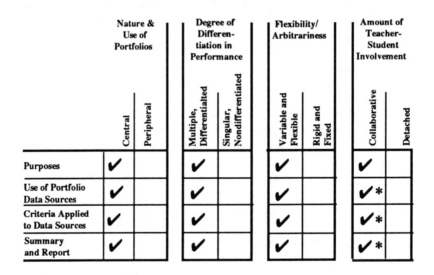

	Nature & Use of Portfolios		Degree of Differentiation in Performance		Flexibility/ Arbitrariness		Amount of Teacher-Student Involvement	
	Central	Peripheral	Multiple, Differentialted	Singular, Nondifferentiated	Variable and Flexible	Rigid and Fixed	Collaborative	Detached
Purposes	✔		✔		✔		✔	
Use of Portfolio Data Sources	✔		✔		✔		✔ *	
Criteria Applied to Data Sources	✔		✔		✔		✔ *	
Summary and Report	✔		✔		✔		✔ *	

*Indicates parents are involved with this aspect of the portfolio process.

Comments

The use of portfolios for evaluation in this classroom represents a concerted effort to involve the students in collaborative evaluations; to pursue evaluation procedures grounded in the students' literacy experiences and their views of their literacy experiences; and to develop the students' self-assessment strategies.

District-Level Portfolio Evaluation Procedure

Background

The large city school district initiated a number of innovative assessment and teaching practices including a holistic assessment of writing using analytical procedures to assess various stylistic and mechanic features of student writing. Teachers were encouraged to use one rubric at all levels in their evaluation of students' writing. Students kept their writing in working folders. Some teachers in the school district initiated their own student portfolios. To complement other assessment data, portfolios are being initiated district-wide at the elementary, middle, and high school level.

Purpose

The district's proposal for evaluating portfolios is intended to serve as a means of broadening the district's writing evaluation to complement holistic writing assessment, and as a means of supporting state mandates for ongoing records of student's strengths and weaknesses. Secondary goals include involving the students in self-assessment.

Process

Schools maintain individual student portfolios, which include:
1. Summative writing samples and scores from the district-wide holistic writing assessment;
2. A representative work sample from each grading period, including a completed self-evaluation form.

Teachers are expected to have a conference periodically with each student for selecting both the writing sample that would be analyzed in accordance with the district's analytic trait rubric and a sample representative of the progress the student makes over the year.

Evaluation Process

Student work is collected in folders provided by the district.

↓

At the end of every quarterly grading period students select their "strongest" draft and complete a self-evaluation of the work to place in their portfolio.

↓

The teacher selects one of the two drafts for formal evaluation using the district's analytic trait rubric.

↓

At the end of the year, when four papers are placed in folder, the student and teacher jointly determine the work that "best reflects the student's growth."

▼

Summative writing assessment scores and samples are added, and the portfolio is passed on to the next year's teacher.

Sources for Evaluation

Writing samples completed in conjunction with classwork as well as writing samples acquired during district-wide writing assessment are used. Scores are derived by applications of the analytic-trait rubric to selected samples.

Criteria for Evaluation

The teacher and students collaborate on the selection of work that represents their best effort and progress over the year. District-level analytic procedures are intended to assess the stylistic and mechanical qualities of individual writing samples.

Summarizing and Reporting

Scores for selected writing samples are generated. In addition, a supplementary evaluation form is completed by the teacher and attached to each student's report card. A copy of this report card is presented in figure 9.2.

Some of the areas included on the report form (e.g., "Writes in a variety of forms"; "Demonstrates ownership of own learning") and the criteria ("Usually"; "Sometimes"; "Working on") tie directly to the portfolio.

Qualitative Analysis of Portfolio Evaluation Procedure

	Nature & Use of Portfolios		Degree of Differentiation in Performance		Flexibility/ Arbitrariness		Amount of Teacher-Student Involvement	
	Central	Peripheral	Multiple, Differentialted	Singular, Nondifferentiated	Variable and Flexible	Rigid and Fixed	Collaborative	Detached
Purposes		✔		✔		✔	✔	
Use of Portfolio Data Sources		✔		✔	✔		✔	
Criteria Applied to Data Sources		✔		✔		✔		✔
Summary and Report		✔		✔		✔		✔

Supplementary Report to Parents
WRITING

This supplementary evaluation form is attached to your child's regular report card in order to supply information that reflects the focus of our instructional program and conforms with our philosophy of education and our school's mission statement.

Explanation of Marks
  U = Usually
  S = Sometimes
  W = Working on

	Grading Period 1	Grading Period 2	Grading Period 3	Grading Period 4
Demonstrates fluency in written expression				
Enjoys and initiates own writing				
Uses own creative ideas in writing				
Develops and organizes ideas				
Writes in a variety of forms				
Uses the writing process				
Communicates clearly in written form				
Shows a willingness to take risks				
Demonstrates ownership of own learning				

Comments:

Grading Period 1 Goal: Demonstrates fluency in written expression.

Grading Period 2 Goal:

Grading Period 3 Goal:

Grading Period 4 Goal:

Figure 9.2: Supplementary Report to Parents

Comments

This district-level proposal represents an attempt to evaluate portfolios in a manner consistent with preexisting views of assessment and evaluation. The portfolios are not the primary means of evaluation but are subordinate to existing goals. Instead of considering the range of possible data that portfolios can yield and the variety of criteria that can be applied, the district proposal is rather restrictive and rigid. Above all, the district proposal forces the portfolio to fit the district's existing analytic scoring procedures. In this regard, the proposal seems to reflect an unwillingness to consider what portfolios might afford and a reluctance to move away from preexisting evaluation procedures. It is as if the district has a limited willingness to consider portfolios.

On the positive side, however, the district has begun to shift its report card to reflect the students' portfolios. In particular, it has included an evaluation of the range of reading and writing the students are pursuing and their degree of ownership. The area of self-evaluation by students has gone undeveloped. The district's goal is to broaden the portfolio approach, including the development of reading portfolios (list of books read, tapes of oral reading, students' published books, reader-response journal entries) as well as teacher observations and assessment. Hopefully, its evaluation procedures will not be limited to the same preexisting procedures, criteria, and strategies that limit the writing portfolio.

A State-level Example

Background

The state of Vermont appears to be about to launch portfolio assessment procedures statewide. The Vermont Commissioner of Education, Richard Mills, describes the evolution of a decision to use portfolios:

> Teacher after teacher argued standardized tests measure a narrow band of performance and trivialize the curriculum... Others insisted there had to to be a test ...[to] show where the money goes... To respond most appropriately to the concern over the lack of statewide assessment, we needed a way to combine the proven familiarity of standardized tests with something that would capture the full range of student performance... We finally hit upon a unique approach, the centerpiece of which is an assessment of performance through a portfolio of student work beginning with writing and mathematics, then expanding into other areas of the curriculum. Also standardized tests, based on Vermont objectives, will provide important anchors (1989, p. 8-9).

Since that decision, the proposal to use portfolios has received funds from the governor and the Governor's Association, approval from the state board of education, and, after lengthy study in committee, support from the state legislature.

Purpose

The Vermont Portfolio plan is intended to address concerns over accountability and the need for assessment data that achieves the following:
1. Informs and enhances curriculum decisions;
2. Spurs examination, reflection, and action on education.

Process

Vermont's portfolio-based evaluation system was piloted in the 1990-91 school year. The plans for 1990-91 were to assess fourth and eighth grade students in writing and mathematics by the use of three methods—a portfolio, a best piece, and a uniform test. In particular, all fourth and eighth grade students will keep portfolios of their "significant work" (papers, poems, extended problems, informative writing, persuasion). The writing portion of the portfolio assessment will contain a minimum of six required pieces that will reflect work across the curriculum. Each piece will be dated, and the portfolio will include all drafts leading to the final product. In addition, each student will select from the portfolio the piece of work that represents his or her best piece of the year. Given that the portfolio is an ongoing part of classroom activities, each portfolio piece as well as the portfolio as a whole will have been assessed by the teacher. A conference with the student is planned to give the student feedback on the portfolio and the criteria used to evaluate it.

Teams of Vermont teachers, trained to evaluate portfolios, will, using a subset of the fourth and eighth grade portfolios, validate the evaluation on the portfolios made by the teacher. In addition, they will score this same set of portfolios against state-established criteria.

Evaluation Process

Guidelines for developing portfolios are implemented.

Students keep collections of various documents (including drafts) of schoolwork and these are dated. Teacher evaluative comments are also kept.

Selected "pieces" including a "best piece" are chosen by the students with the teacher's help.

▼

Self-evaluative comments as well as teachers evaluative comments are included with the portfolio document.

▼

Teacher evaluates "whole" portfolio and gives feedback to students.

▼

Trained, outside reviewers randomly select a subset of portfolios that are evaluated in accordance with state adopted criteria and guidelines.

▼

Summary report for portfolios is provided for schools and programs. Schools share portfolio-based report with community and discuss plans for improvement.

▼

With staff support, plans for improvement are pursued.

Sources for Evaluation

The minimum content for the Vermont writing portfolios is as follows:
1. Table of contents;
2. "Best piece" (dated, chosen with teacher's help, all drafts);
3. Letters to reviewers explaining choice of "best piece" and process of development;
4. Poem, short story, or play (dated, all drafts);
5. Content area prose piece (dated, all drafts);
6. Personal, written response to a book, current issue, social problem, math problem or scientific phenomena (dated, all drafts).

For purposes of state-level evaluation, a random sample of student portfolios is collected.

Criteria for Evaluation

The guidelines for evaluating portfolios is accomplished with established criteria applied to a random set of portfolios from a grade level. The following two sets of criteria are applied to the portfolio by the outside reviewers:
1. A set of criteria for evaluating individual student portfolios and "best pieces";
2. A set of criteria for evaluating the program representing the portfolio set.

Figure 9.3 lists the criteria or guidelines used to evaluate individual portfolios; Figure 9.4 lists the criteria or guidelines used to evaluate portfolios across a program.

Figure 9.3 Criteria for Individual Portfolios

1.   *Does the writing exhibit sentence variety and a sense of personal expression?*
[] Unacceptable [] Low Acceptable [] High Acceptable [] Outstanding

2.   *Does the final draft exhibit an awareness of appropriate mechanics, usage and grammar?*
[] Unacceptable [] Low Acceptable [] High Acceptable [] Outstanding

3.   *Is there a sense of fluency and organization suitable to the writer's purpose?*
[] Unacceptable [] Low Acceptable [] High Acceptable [] Outstanding

4.   *Does the writer attempt significant revision and is there evidence of improvement from the first draft to the final copy?*
[] Unacceptable [] Low Acceptable [] High Acceptable [] Outstanding
[] N/A: Writer's submitted work demonstrates first draft work at "final draft" level.

Figure 9.4: Criteria for Program

1.   *Development of student: Is there progress from earliest dated to most recently dated works?*
[] Unacceptable [] Low Acceptable [] High Acceptable [] Outstanding

2.   *Range of writing: Is there evidence of sufficient variety to challenge all students and to allow each student an opportunity for success?*
[] Unacceptable [] Low Acceptable [] High Acceptable [] Outstanding

3.   *Breadth/intensity of responses to the writing: How much evidence is there of teacher/peer response to the student's drafts, and opportunity for revision by the student?*
[] Unacceptable [] Low Acceptable [] High Acceptable [] Outstanding

Summarizing and Reporting

The strengths and weaknesses of portfolios as determined by the various criteria are transformed into a summary report. This report lists the extent to which various "best pieces" and "portfolios" are acceptable—outstanding or low acceptability or unacceptable—and provides an overall summary of the report. An example of such a report is included in Figure 9.5.

VERMONT STATEWIDE WRITING ASSESSMENT:

NAME OF SCHOOL: ALL THINGS UNION SCHOOL (K-12)
YEAR OF REPORT: 1990-91

GRADE REPORTED: 4TH
NUMBER OF CLASSROOMS REPORTED: 4
TOTAL NUMBER OF 4TH GRADE STUDENTS IN SAMPLE: 34

1. Sentence variety and sense of personal expression:

	Best piece	Portfolio
% of students "Unacceptable"	_____	_____
% of students "Low acceptable"	_____	_____
% of students "High acceptable"	_____	_____
% of students "Outstanding"	_____	_____

2. Mechanics, usage and grammar:

% of students "Unacceptable"	_____	_____
% of students "Low acceptable"	_____	_____
% of students "High acceptable"	_____	_____
% of students "Outstanding"	_____	_____

3. Fluency and organization:

% of students "Unacceptable"	_____	_____
% of students "Low acceptable"	_____	_____
% of students "High acceptable"	_____	_____
% of students "Outstanding"	_____	_____

4. Revision, improvement from 1st draft to final copy:

% of students "Unacceptable"	_____	_____
% of students "Low acceptable"	_____	_____
% of students "High acceptable"	_____	_____
% of students "Outstanding"	_____	_____

PROGRAM EVALUATION:

1. Development of Students:

% of students "Unacceptable"	_____
% of students "Low acceptable"	_____
% of students "High acceptable"	_____
% of students "Outstanding"	_____

2. Range of writing challenges:

% of students "Unacceptable"	_____
% of students "Low acceptable"	_____
% of students "High acceptable"	_____
% of students "Outstanding"	_____

3. Breadth/intensity of focus on each assignment:

% of students "Unacceptable"	_____
% of students "Low acceptable"	_____
% of students "High acceptable"	_____
% of students "Outstanding"	_____

REVIEWERS' COMMENTS: Fourth graders at this school have a strong grasp of mechanics, and the fluency in their papers demonstrates that most of them write frequently: They are well practiced. The high percentage of students whose work never goes beyond a first draft suggests that the school might want to make a greater effort at encouraging students to revise their work. Responses from teachers in three of the four classrooms were designed to encourage the students but did not provide direction for future work. We commend the teacher of class 4D and encourage the school to review the way this teacher responds to student work. None of the portfolios reviewed contained work from content areas other than Language Arts. We exhort teachers to foster writing in all content areas.

Figure 9.5: Summary

Schools will report the results to their communities on school report day, and the state will report the result in its report on the condition of education. In partnership with the state, schools will plan to initiate improvements based upon these reports.

Qualitative Analysis of Portfolio Evaluation Procedure

	Nature & Use of Portfolios		Degree of Differentiation in Performance		Flexibility/ Arbitrariness		Amount of Teacher-Student Involvement	
	Central	Peripheral	Multiple, Differentiated	Singular, Nondifferentiated	Variable and Flexible	Rigid and Fixed	Collaborative	Detached
Purposes	✔		✔			✔	✔	
Use of Portfolio Data Sources	✔		✔		✔		✔	
Criteria Applied to Data Sources	✔		✔			✔		✔
Summary and Report	✔		✔			✔		✔

Arts PROPEL

Background

Arts PROPEL, a five-year cooperative project, is funded by the Arts and Humanities Division of the Rockefeller Foundation and involves artists, researchers, and educators from Harvard Project Zero, the Educational Testing Service, and the Pittsburgh public school system. Believing that those educated in an art form should be able to express themselves in that form, comprehend and appreciate art from different cultures, and reflect on features of production and perception in that form, Arts PROPEL focuses on three areas—music, visual arts, and imaginative writing. Through the use of two educational vehicles, domain projects and portfolios, Arts PROPEL is exploring tools that provide a record of artistic growth and development as well as acccurate authentic curriculum based assessment (Portfolio, 1989).

Purpose

Participants in Arts PROPEL believe that there is no single

right way to use portfolios and, therefore, suggest that it is first important to consider what portfolios are being asked to accomplish. They suggest that a portfolio is more than the work it contains, its strength lies in the process of how it is used. Portfolios become evidence of growth and change over time in terms of reflection, involvement in long-term projects, self-concept, and visual awareness.

Process

Portfolios in the Arts PROPEL project are a developmental process in which students become the center of the assessment process and are asked to provide answers to questions about their strengths, weaknesses and improvements. Students are expected to explore their discipline, maintain long-term interest, and develop in the artistic process. Portfolios become a forum for their creative expression and provide evidence of their growth in terms of production, perception, and reflection.

Norman Brown, an Arts PROPEL art teacher, discusses several important components of this process: the portfolio review, pivitol pieces, companion pieces, and footprints (Brown, 1989). The portfolio review is continual and occurs on an ongoing basis, providing students with the opportunity to discuss their ideas freely and become apart of the evaluation process. Pivotal pieces are those that have "provided students with new insight or sense of direction." Companion pieces are two-fold: they can be pieces that developed as an outgrowth of class critique or are projects that involve the same idea constructed in different ways. Footprints involve returning to pieces done in the past and a willingness to continue working on and refining the piece. As Brown suggests, each of these components engage students in their work and the assessment process.

Process of Evaluation

While there appears to be no standard portfolio process within Arts PROPEL, a look at the phases outlined by Kathryn Howard provides a framework for PROPEL portfolios (Howard, 1990).

Modeling and oral reflection: Students collect work. Students begin to think of themselves as writers. Teacher models response to reflection questions.

↓

First written reflection are produced by students.

↓

Portfolios begin: Student selects important piece. Student responds to reflection questions about the piece.

↓

Portfolio update: Student selects both a satisfying and an unsatisfying piece. Student responds to reflection questions about the pieces.

↓

Finalizing portfolio: Students review the entire body of their work. Students are given opportunity to replace a selection. Students respond to reflection questions about any replaced piece.

Sources for Evaluation

It is difficult to compile a list of sources for Arts PROPEL portfolios because they cover a wide range of disciplines. Arts PROPEL portfolios reflect the work of musicians, playwrites, choreographers, dancers, artists, and writers. Below is a listing of generic sources that could apply to any Arts PROPEL portfolio:

- Finished pieces;
- Pivotal pieces;
- Companion pieces;
- Journals—student reflections;
- Work in process or progress;
- Videotapes;
- Audiotapes;
- Class discussions;
- Peer reflections.

Criteria for Evaluation

As with all aspects of PROPEL portfolios, criteria for evaluation varies depending on the need or purpose of the portfolio. Listed below are possible criteria for evaluation as outlined by Steve Seidel (Seidel, 1989).

- Number of writing opportunities in a new genre;
- Investigation of accomplished work in an area;
- Collaborating with peers;
- Sharing work;
- Assessment of one's own work;
- Revision.

Summarizing and Reporting

Believing that at this point the most important function of curriculum-based assessment is the establishment of a "portfolio culture," little has been written about the summarizing and reporting of PROPEL portfolios. This remains an area for more development.

Qualitative Analysis of Portfolio Evaluation Procedure

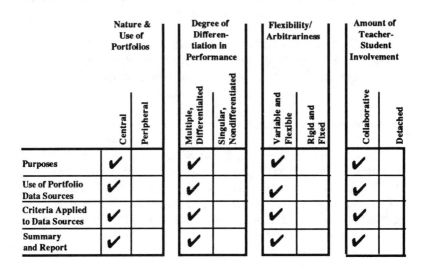

	Nature & Use of Portfolios		Degree of Differentiation in Performance		Flexibility/ Arbitrariness		Amount of Teacher-Student Involvement	
	Central	Peripheral	Multiple, Differentialted	Singular, Nondifferentiated	Variable and Flexible	Rigid and Fixed	Collaborative	Detached
Purposes	✔		✔		✔		✔	
Use of Portfolio Data Sources	✔		✔		✔		✔	
Criteria Applied to Data Sources	✔		✔		✔		✔	
Summary and Report	✔		✔		✔		✔	

Comments

As is evident from this overview of the Arts PROPEL project, it is difficult to define or develop a single PROPEL portfolio, and we believe this to be one of the many strengths of the project. A portfolio is not a static tool but one that is meant to be fluid to meet the needs of students and teachers. PROPEL portfolios provide a forum for creative experimentation as well as a tool for assessment of growth and development. They encourage collaboration and foster learning and reflection. It will, therefore, be interesting to watch the growth and development of PROPEL portfolios and the continual growth of the "portfolio culture" within PROPEL classrooms.

Stanford Teacher Assessment Portfolios

Background

The Stanford Teacher Assessment portfolio project represents a unique use of portfolios as an evaluation tool. Whereas the major focus of our book is the evaluation of student reading-writing portfolios, we feel the Stanford portfolio evaluation procedures were sufficiently unique and innovative to merit inclusion.

The main goal of the Stanford project was to develop criteria for teacher certification. With this in mind, it focused on specific areas (e.g., integrated language arts) for which it explored the possibility of teachers documenting their instruction with portfolios and the viability of establishing criteria and strategies for evaluating these portfolios in terms of meriting teacher certification.

A unique aspect of the Stanford proposal was the degree to which the team asked themselves ongoing questions about the data sources they needed, the criteria that might be applied, and the extent to which the assessment and evaluation should and can be collaborative. As a research and development effort, the Stanford initiative is exemplary in terms of the ways in which it has pursued the ongoing refinement of a portfolio evaluation process.

Purpose

The Stanford Portfolio Evaluation for teachers represents a research and development effort which has focused on identifying usable ways a portfolio-based evaluation process can assess the quality of teaching practice in conjunction with making judgments as to whether or not a teacher should be certified.

Process

There are several strands to the Stanford project. For our purposes, we have focused on the elementary literacy strand in which differentiated criteria for teachers representing alternative approaches (e.g., integrated language arts versus traditional language arts) have been developed. We will describe the procedures for evaluating the portfolios of teachers representing integrated language arts.

The teachers are asked to identify their planning and interaction for three-to-five weeks of integrated language arts. In particular, teachers are asked to show evidence of areas deemed important points of emphasis for an integrated language arts orientation:

1. Literature anchors the plans;
2. The language arts (reading, writing, speaking, and listening) are integrated;
3. Lessons reveal a linking of concepts and skills over time;
4. Individual differences (cultural, language, ability, prior knowledge) are assessed;
5. Desired outcomes are pursued.

To this end, teachers are provided with a 'checklist that itemizes the required portfolio documents (see Figure 9.6).

INTEGRATED LANGUAGE INSTRUCTION: CHECKLIST

I. <u>Entry One</u>:   Planning and Adapting Instruction

__A. <u>OVERVIEW</u>:   one-to-three page overview of plans for three-to-five weeks of integrated language instruction

__B. <u>LESSON PLANS</u>:   detailed plans for three constructive days of lessons

__C. <u>LIST OF LITERATURE SELECTIONS</u>:   list of selections used during the period of instruction, with brief annotations providing reasons for choices

__D. <u>JOURNAL EXCERPTS</u>:   three excerpts from journal that describe adaptations made as instruction proceeded and reasons for changes from the advance planning

__E. <u>REFLECTIVE STATEMENT</u>:   A one-to-two page statement about what happened during   implementation of plans (See Handbook, page 48 for more details)

II. <u>Entry Two</u>:   Teaching Integrated Language Arts

__A. <u>VIDEOTAPE OF INTEGRATED LANGUAGE INSTRUCTION</u>

____1. A large-group lesson dealing with literature

____2. A small-group discussion of a literature selection, from ten-to-fifteen minutes in length using four to eight student participants

____3. Two one-to-one writing conferences, using students with diverse literacy needs

__B. <u>STATEMENT OF PURPOSE</u>:   brief statement describing purpose of each videotaped lesson, including intended student learning. Handbook, page 51 ("Document the circumstances...") describes some optional information you may want to include regarding special circumstances of videotaped lesson or class

__C. <u>SAMPLES OF STUDENT WORK</u>:   items produced during a lesson, with caption attached

__D. <u>COPIES OF HANDOUTS</u>:   handouts, boardwork notes, or any other aids used during videotaped lessons (OPTIONAL)

__E. <u>VIDEOTAPE ANALYSIS</u>:   one-to-two page written or short audiotaped analysis of videotaped lesson(s) (OPTIONAL)

_F. <u>OBSERVATION NOTES</u>:   notes from an outsider's observation of your teaching by mentor, advisor, administrator, etc.   (OPTIONAL)

Figure 9.6: Integrated Language Instruction Checklist

Once the documentation is gathered the material is subjected to several reviews, including some by both an external reviewer and the teacher collaboratively. The first review is directed at identifying the data sources that offered evidence of the aforementioned features. (See Figure 9.7)

Figure 9.7: Matrix of Performance Criteria

ENTRY ONE: PLANNING AND ADAPTING

Mark an X in appropriate spots.

Portfolio Documents

CRITERIA	Overview	Lesson Plans	Literature Selections	Journal Excerpts	Reflective Statement	Student Work *	Handouts *	Other *
Planning								
(1) Integration of language arts								
(2) Cohesive links								
(3) Grounding in appropriate literature								
Adapting & Tailoring								
(4) Reader-text links								
(5) Culturally diverse literature								
(6) Adapting to student needs								

* Optional documents

Matrix of Performance Criteria:
Integrated Language Instruction

ENTRY TWO: TEACHING

Portfolio Documents

CRITERIA	Statements of purpose	Videotape: Large-group Discussion	Videotape: Small-group Discussion	Video/Audiotape: Writing Conferences	Student Work Samples	Videotape Analysis	Handouts	Other::
Orchestrating Purposeful Plans								
(A) Clear purposes								
(B) Moving students through activities								
(C) Variety of group sizes								
Discussion Leading								
(A) Encouraging student participation								
(B) Monitoring discussion								
(C) Student involvement								
Interpretation & Critical Thinking								
(A) Helping students think critically								
(B) Dignifying multiple interpretations								
Working with Writing								
(A) Scaffolding								
(B) Response & revision								

The second review is intended to evaluate each portfolio quantitatively and qualitatively. (See Figure 9.8) The final prompt on the page is intended as an advance organizer for a future review that is carried out in conference with the teacher. This conference may involve having the teacher do the following:

1. Expand on some element of the portfolio;
2. Clarify the purpose of intended student outcome;
3. Identify the support provided students in a learning episode;
4. Address a perceived deficiency.

Figure 9.8: Characterizing the Portfolio Entry Chart

CHARACTERIZING THE PORTFOLIO ENTRY: ENTRY ONE: PLANNING

INSTRUCTIONS: Circle the number for the most appropriate characterization and fill in pertinent information below.

Criterion 1: Integration of the Language Arts. Plans were effectively organized to integrate the language arts (reading, writing, speaking, and listening), rather than treat them in isolation.

1   UNACCEPTABLE.
Even for a novice, these lessons, fraught with errors or problems, are badly conceived, disorganized, misinformed.

2   WEAK.
Evidence of only one or two language arts in use; language arts appear to be treated in isolation. Acceptable only for a novice. Teacher will likely need much help with this criterion.

3   AVERAGE.
Language arts appear to be fairly well integrated for teaching concepts, themes, skills. Plans are reasonably well conceived and organized, but are not of Board Certification calibre.

4   IMPRESSIVE.
Clear evidence that the teacher integrates all four language arts to teach concepts, themes, skills. Teacher extends student learning and practice from one language art into other language arts. Plans well informed and conceived. Board Certification calibre.

> EXAMPLE: The teacher reads an excerpt aloud from a book then poses for students a question to be explored in small discussion groups: after students discuss responses in groups, they write responses individually then return to full class to read some responses aloud.

5   OUTSTANDING.
Beyond the qualities suggested for a rating of 4, the lessons include exceptional insight, creativity, energy, or grace that clearly exceeds Board expectations.

(1)   Which document(s)/evidence support the rating? (e.g.Lesson Plan #2)

(2)   How does the evidence justify the rating?

(3)   Qualifications:

     (a)   Special strengths of the performance for this criterion:

     (b)   "Flags," problems, concerns:

     (c)   Areas to probe in Assessment Center Follow-Up Interview?

Evaluation process

Goals of portfolio evaluation including criteria and
documentation guidelines are presented.

▼

Teacher gathers documentations and annotations
(think-alouds, explanatory notes, etc.).

▼

Teacher portfolios are reviewed to assess the documents
that can be used to evaluate teachers.

▼

Portfolios are evaluated in terms of criteria. Checklists are
completed and written comments are developed.

▼

Teacher reviewer conferences are held to clarify, to
obtain further information, and to offer to feed back
to teachers and reviewers.

Sources for Evaluation

The teacher portfolio for evaluation involves documentation of three to five weeks of instruction. To this end, they are encouraged to provide:

1. An overview of the three to five weeks,
2. Detailed plans of three consecutive days of lesson plans, as well as
3. Various other support such as audiotapes of planning conferences, captions or documents, samples of student work, their own think-alouds, teacher explanations together with accompanying student work. A listing of some of these sources is included in Figure 9.6.

Criteria for Evaluation

Drawing from observations of talented teachers, research, and experience with the portfolios, the Stanford research group generated a list of features for which the teachers are expected to provide documentation and a listing of performance criteria related to these features. In evaluating each teacher's portfolio on these criteria, they examine the different portfolio documents as well as hold conferences with the teacher.

Summarizing and reporting

Checklists and written comments are the primary means used to summarize and report the teacher performance.

Qualitative Analysis of Portfolio Evaluation:

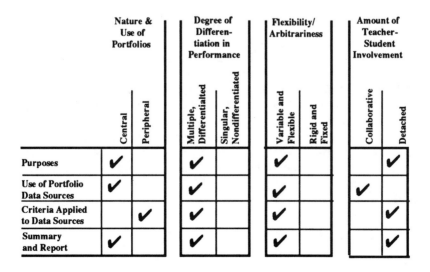

	Nature & Use of Portfolios		Degree of Differentiation in Performance		Flexibility/ Arbitrariness		Amount of Teacher-Student Involvement	
	Central	Peripheral	Multiple, Differentialted	Singular, Nondifferentiated	Variable and Flexible	Rigid and Fixed	Collaborative	Detached
Purposes	✔		✔		✔			✔
Use of Portfolio Data Sources	✔		✔		✔		✔	
Criteria Applied to Data Sources		✔	✔		✔			✔
Summary and Report	✔		✔		✔			✔

Comments

The Stanford Evaluation procedures represent an attempt to use portfolios as a primary source of documentation and a grounded evaluation of teachers. Above all, it does not assume that portfolios will be totally similar nor does it assume that the evidence of effectiveness is tied to documentation established *a priori*. Furthermore, the approach to the evaluation is somewhat collaborative. The teachers choose the material to be included in the portfolio; however the teacher is not included in the actual evaluation of these materials. In terms of the proposal's limitations, it is unfortunate that the criteria that they have thoughtfully developed do not allow for more variation. Along with the development of criteria, a decision was made to implement the use of a single set standard across all portfolios rather than to apply different standards to different portfolios. The standard that evolved was tied to California State Department guidelines. While we would argue that menu of possible criteria would have been more reasonable, the Stanford group seemed to view such as difficult to manage.

Discussion of Portfolio Evaluation

It was our hope that this chapter would answer the question: How might portfolios be used to evaluate student portfolios? We have presented a number of different models that have emerged from classroom teachers, district-level personnel, state departments and university-level researchers. We hope the models gave you an appreciation of the possibilities and that this information reinforced the fact that not all portfolio evaluation procedures are equal. Implicit in the framework we have used to discuss the various portfolio evaluation proposals are some biases that you have probably discovered.

We favor an approach to portfolio evaluation that is primary, central to the life of the classroom, multiple and differentiating, variable and flexible, and, above all, collaborative. Portfolios can be dynamic vehicles for student self-evaluation. We hope that the evaluation is grounded in documents that reflect the range of "real" literacy effort of students rather than those restricted and rather constrained responses evaluated using formal indices. In essence, some of the proposals described in this chapter are "portfolios in name only." The pursuit of simplification, standardization, and objectivity for portfolio evaluation seems contrary to actual portfolios that are by nature complex, individual, and subjective.

Some Related Concerns

We are often asked by teachers about student involvement

and how to proceed: is it empowering or overwhelming for students to be asked to sit down with their portfolio and to arrive at an appropriate formal assessment not only for their achievement but also for their process, effort, progress, and attitude? How can we expect children to adequately and competently assess their own work? Are we, as teachers, abdicating our role if we encourage students to help to establish the criteria by which their work will be assessed and then encourage them to apply those criteria to their own portfolios?

The answer is that it is far more overwhelming for students to sit by passively while their work is being evaluated by what appears to them to be a series of arbitrary and incomprehensible standards established independently of the work being assessed. We have found that when given the opportunity, it is the students who are the most perceptive judges of their own work because it is the students who best know the intricacies involved in the formulation of the portfolios. It is the students, in conjunction with teachers, parents and peers, who have struggled with the compilation of the portfolio. Assessment is not an isolated responsibility for the teacher, but a collaborative effort designed to inform not only the teacher's instruction but also the students' learning. As such we believe that it is essential to involve the students in actively developing criteria and assessing their own portfolios.

How often should the students be asked to assess their portfolios formally? In a large measure this depends on the organization of the individual classroom, the number of times students are asked to review the entire body of their work, selecting favorite or representative pieces, and the needs of individual students. In many classrooms showcase portfolios are assembled and assessed on a quarterly basis, enabling students and parents to better understand the grades reflected on the report card. In some cases it is the student who decides that there are several new pieces that represent growth and change to be included in the portfolio. Since informal self-assessment is occurring on an on-going basis, students are well aware of their own growth and progress.

For the students it is this ongoing informal assessment that enables them to become active participants in more formal assessment practices. On a daily basis students are encouraged to examine their work in process, to compare it to previous pieces, and to analyze their purpose for writing, their perspective, and their audience. They are asked to consider their effort and to discuss the strengths and weaknesses in their work. In conjunction with their teachers and peers, they are asked to establish for themselves a concept of a good reader and writer and the skills involved in the process, and then to develop personal goals for becoming readers and writers themselves.

Daily, they are asked to measure themselves against their own goals and to revise those goals as they mature and develop and discover their strengths as well as the areas in which they still need work.

For these students formal assessment becomes an extension of a daily process, perhaps in a more institutionalized format. Again that format varies depending on the needs of the student and teacher. As we have suggested, in some cases students are asked to write a paragraph that gives their overall opinion of their portfolio in terms of their effort, progress, achievement, attitudes, and goals. They are asked to include in the summary an indication of improvement and change and to cite examples. Students might be given a checklist to ensure that they cover criteria important to themselves as well as the teacher and then be asked to assess each of the criteria on a predetermined scale. Such a scale could include categories such as little evidence, evidence, and much evidence in the portfolio and then ask for specific examples and explanations. Often assessment scales are differentiated for effort and achievement. In some cases a formalized scale could be quantified, allowing the student to arrive at an overall score, much like an holistic assessment.

Regardless of the system used, we have found that students are an important component in the evaluation process. As collaborators rather than participants, students are empowered to evaluate their own processes and products, their own strengths and needs as readers and writers, and as a result they grow in skill, knowledge and confidence and are more likely to become lifelong learners. Giving students the opportunity to be collaborators in the assessment of their choices and their learning allows the grading process to become a tool for learning and for the development of further goals.

We are often asked to address the ways in which parents respond to portfolios. In our experience, parents have preferred portfolios over standardized test results. Furthermore, portfolios invite parents to take an active role in their children's evaluative experiences. Parents can be an extremely important component in their children's learning process. We have found that beyond possessing a concern for their children's growth and development, parents can become active participants in their children's learning. Prior to formal schooling it is often solely the parents who know and can discuss their children's strengths and weaknesses in terms of language acquisition or their likes and dislikes regarding books and favorite characters. All too often, with the advent of formal schooling, parents can lose the intimate knowledge they have of their children's language development. A child's triumph in reading is noted by an "A" but does not reflect the wide range of different genres the child has sampled. However, portfolios not only allow parents to continue their involvement in their children's language growth, they can also allow them to become participants in the assessment process.

In many classrooms parents have become important links in the assessment of their children's showcase portfolios. This serves a three-fold purpose in that parents not only see a wide range of their children's work but also, learn how their children view their own work and the criteria by which they are assessed. In such a system, where parents see a vast array of their children's work on a continual basis, they are immediately aware of problems or concerns and can work with the teacher and their children to arrive at appropriate solutions.

There are many ways parents can serve as partners in the assessment process, particularly when they have a strong overall sense of their children's work. On a daily basis parents serve as an audience for work in process. Parents can serve as reviewers for a particular finished product or for an entire showcase portfolio. They can be asked to note growth and change or to comment on content or voice. They can note lists of books read and can encourage their children to experience a different author or a new genre.

However, we have found that it is essential that this is not done in isolation. It is important that portfolios are carefully explained to the parents and that criteria for evaluation are shared with them. For many teachers a private conference spent reviewing a portfolio in process has become an excellent tool for explaining not only the portfolio but also the parents' role. For other teachers a letter sent home with the port-

folio documents the importance placed in the portfolio, the parents' role, and the criteria by which parents are asked to view the work.

The number of times parents are involved in this formal assessment of their child's portfolio will vary with the individual classroom, as will the particular form of evaluation. Some teachers ask that the parents review and comment on the entire portfolio, while others prefer that parents comment on the piece that the student has determined to be the best.

The evaluations themselves will, also, vary across classrooms. In some cases parents are asked to write brief comments that note achievement, effort, process, growth, and change. In others, they are provided with a basic holistic scoring guide and are asked to assess on the criteria noted. In still other classrooms, parents are asked to discuss with their children their individual goals and plans and then to comment on the portfolio on the basis of those individual goals.

However portfolios are developed and used in the classroom, parents can serve an important role in the assessment process, and the portfolio itself can provide the link that draws the parents into the classroom and into their children's work. As a result, report card grades will be more relevant to the parents, and their understanding of the process of their children's learning will aid in the children's growth and development. Again, the collaborative nature of assessment will have allowed parents to become a part of the learning process, and assessment will have become a tool for instruction rather than an isolated report.

A Final Word

The bulk of the testing that occurs yearly in classrooms are the state mandated achievement tests. It has been estimated that over the course of a school year at least fourteen hours are spent preparing students for standardized tests, and this does not account for the time actually spent taking the tests. It is, also, not clear that such tests actually give policy makers appropriate information regarding student progress and achievement. Why, therefore, do we spend precious classroom time asking our students to take such tests? Is there a viable alternative that will better fulfill the goals of standardized testing without necessitating such a large additional allocation of classroom time and effort?

For the most part standardized tests are touted as the best and most efficient way to provide accountability to stakeholders. While individualized reports are essential on a classroom level, schools, districts and states are looking for the aggregate reporting of performance. Policy makers want to see documented the overall picture of a large group of students. Such information aids in their policy decisions, as well as their analysis of program effectiveness, and provides assurance that students are achieving appropriate standards. It is, therefore, essential if curriculum is to be developed that is responsive to students' needs and provides direction for instruction, that teachers report valid information on how students are achieving over time. The summarizing and reporting of students' achievement must be consistent with and reflect what we know to be the process of students' learning. It must be an appropriate representation of the way teachers and students collaboratively develop and inform instruction.

Portfolios not only provide insight into individual student learning, they can also serve to provide aggregate information for schools, districts, and states. Already documented within a portfolio is evidence of the standards being met by children. An overview of the portfolios of an entire grade level will provide immediate information about program effectiveness.

Articles and Papers
about Portfolios

Athanases, S. Dolan, J., Dillon, D. (1989). *Problems in the assessment of teacher portfolios of integrated language arts instruction.* Paper presented at American Educational Research Association Annual Meeting, San Francisco, CA.
> The authors describe the Stanford Teacher Assessment project, which incorporates the use of teacher portfolio for teacher evaluation. The paper describes the procedures for developing and evaluating the portfolios of language arts teachers as well as the problems involved.

Au, K. (1990). *From tests to portfolios: Exploring assumptions about literacy assessment.* Paper presented at the National Reading Conference, Miami, FL.
> Comparisons are made across teachers who use portfolios and those who choose not to do so. She traces their assumptions and beliefs and how those views shifted for those who used portfolios.

Bingham, A. (1988). "Using writing folders to document student progress." In T. Newkirk and N. Atwell (Eds.), *Understanding writing: Ways of observing, learning, and teaching* (2nd ed.), pp. 216-225. Portsmouth, NH: Heinemann.
> Suggesting that documenting progress is the primary focus of writing folders, Bingham discusses how the folder can become an important teaching tool, as well as a resource in parent education. Through a series of examples, she demonstrates how a writing folder coupled with a teacher's notes can document student's growth and development over an academic year.

Brandt, R. (December, 1987/January, 1988). On assessment in the arts: A conversation with Howard Gardner. *Educational Leadership, 45,* (4), 30-34.
> Through the use of an interview format, Harvard's Project Zero is discussed with Howard Gardner. Gardner indicates that in assessing aesthetic growth three kinds of things are monitored: production, perception, and reflection. He stresses that in this program students learn by doing rather than imitating, as can be demonstrated through their portfolios, which are envisioned as a "data base," allowing students and teachers to see what has actually been accomplished.

Brown, N. (1987). Pivotal pieces. *Portfolio, 1,* (2), 9-13.

Brown, a visual arts specialist in the Pittsburgh Public Schools involved with Arts PROPEL, traces the growth of his understanding of the use of portfolios and of their significance in students' growth and development. For him portfolios have become more than a collection of students' work; portfolios involve students in the perception and reflection of their work. Using his students' own pieces, he cites the significance of the students' preliminary sketches, or "pivotal pieces," in their understanding of their own growth and development.

Brown, N. (1989) Portfolio review: Pivots, companions and footprints *Portfolio, 1*, (4) 8-11.

Brown, an Arts PROPEL art teacher, discusses learning as a developmental process involving students in finding their own answers to their strengths, weaknesses, and improvements and necessitating the use of portfolios   He reflects on several important components of this process—the ongoing portfolio review, the use of "pivotal pieces" to provide new insight and direction for students, the use of a "series" or "companion pieces" to show the development of a set of ideas, and the use of "footprints" or the ability to reexamine old ideas and trace learning and development.

Camp, R. (1990). *Integrating testing, teaching and learning.* Paper presented at the annual meeting of the International Reading Association, Atlanta, GA.

Camp traces the nature and role of portfolios in conjunction with describing the Arts PROPEL portfolio project and providing a forum for comparing traditional assessment with portfolio assessment.

Camp, R. (1990). Thinking together about portfolios.*The Quarterly, 12*, (2), 8-14, 27.

In this article Camp, a researcher from the Educational Testing Service working with the Arts PROPEL project, presents a retrospective of the collaborative development of PROPEL writing portfolios. She discusses the thinking that prompted the use of that portfolios, the development of the portfolios themselves, and the environment that fostered their growth. Camp also focuses on and discusses a key component of the Arts PROPEL classrooms, the series of activities and procedures that help students create portfolios and leads to an ongoing reflection of their work.

Carr, B. (1987, March). Portfolios. *School Arts, 86* , 55-56.

A portfolio that provides a record of accomplishments and skills is an essential requirement for those working in the visual arts. Carr provides suggestions for the creation and layout of a student's first portfolio.

Carter, M., & Tierney, R. J. (1988). *Reading and writing growth: Using portfolios in assessment.* Paper presented at National Reading Conference, Tucson, AZ.

The authors describe the impact of portfolios upon teachers and students in different classrooms. Specifically, they present the findings of a study that examines how teachers' awareness of students, teaching practices and students' views of themselves as readers and writers shifted in conjunction with their use of portfolios.

Chapman, L. H. (1978). *Approaches to art in education.* New York: Harcourt Brace Jovanovich, 392-399.

Given the belief that evaluation should be an integral part of the learning process, this section of the text discusses important factors to be considered when evaluating a student, including methods of obtaining records, interpretation of the materials collected, and reporting that information to others.

Collins, A. (1990). Portfolios for assessing student learning in science: A new name for a familiar idea? In A.B. Champagne, B.E. Lovitts, & B.E. Callinger.(Eds.), *Assessment in the service of instruction.* Washington, DC: American Association for the Advancement of Science.

> Collins provides an overview of portfolios in terms of three important features—the purpose, the context and the design, and suggests that these features will change in accordance with teachers' and students' needs. While suggesting that portfolios will differ from discipline to discipline, he provides excellent examples of how portfolios can be used across grade levels in the science classroom.

Educational Testing Service (1989). *The student writer: An endangered species?* Focus 23. Princeton, NJ: Education Testing Service.

> This pamphlet contains brief but good summaries of writing as a process, writing portfolios, writing across the curriculum, and whole language instruction. It evaluates and discusses the effectiveness of these processes using research that is short-term and that does not reflect a student-centered approach to either portfolios or assessment.

Educational Testing Service (1990). *Reading framework: 1992 National Assessment of Educational Progress reading assessment consensus planning project.*

> This explores the shifts in assessment in literacy and discusses the ramifications for future NAEP assessments. Among the proposals discussed and outlined is the introduction of portfolio-based assessment for reading. To this end, they describe the need for a study of actual classroom work in reading.

Elbow, P., & Belanoff, P. (1986). Portfolios as a substitute for proficiency examinations. *College Composition and Communication, 37,* (3), 336-339.

> Believing that proficiency exams were not the way to document proficiency with the writing process, the State University of New York at Stony Brook adopted the portfolio as the method of assessment for their required writing course. In this article Elbow and Belanoff describe the portfolio system as it worked for them in terms of its effect on students' writing, the roles developed between student and teacher, and the collaboration encouraged and developed among teachers.

Evans, K. & Vavrus, L. (1990). *The role of document captions in student portfolios as a link between teacher and student assessment.* Paper presented at National Reading Conference, Miami, FL.

> The authors focus on the nature and role of teacher reflections via captions on documents included in student portfolios. Their findings suggest that such captions reveal the teacher's knowledge, and decision-making and serve as a vehicle for linking assessment to teaching.

Farr, R. & Lowe, K. (1990). *Alternative assessment in language arts.* Paper presented at the National Symposium on Alternative Assessment, Indiana University, Bloomington, IN.

> This paper discusses guidelines for assessment, the use of portfolios as a example of assessment that meets these objectives, and issues (philosophical, political, implementation) surrounding alternative assessment

Flood, J., & Lapp, D. (1989). Reporting reading progress: A comparison portfolio for parents. *The Reading Teacher, 42,* (7), 508-514.

> Flood and Lapp describe the portfolio as a tool to be used in parent conferences to document student change across time. They suggest that a single score fails to report progress accurately. A portfolio should contain not only grades, norm, and criterion reference tests, but also

informal measures that provide examples of progress. They document how these informal measures might be collected and suggest possible interpretations for use with parents.

Galleher, D. (1987). Assessment in context: Toward a national writing project model. *The Quarterly, 9,* (3), 5-7.

Through a hypothetical situation Galleher documents many of the problems students face when states attempt to implement large-scale assessment in writing without consulting those directly involved in instruction. He concludes by suggesting that portfolio assessment can offer a more valid measure of a student's ability than the score from a single test, and he highlights the role of the National Writing Project in attempting to develop more appropriate large-scale assessment.

George, J. E. (1990) *Portfolio assessment: Monitoring teacher change through video-tape.* Paper presented at the National Reading Conference, Miami, FL.

This paper reports the ways that teachers were able to use video-tapes in their portfolios to implement strategies in micro-teaching simulations and in their own classrooms.

Howard, K. (1990). Making the writing portfolio real. *The Quarterly, 12* (2), 4-7, 27.

As a member of the PROPEL writing team, a collaborative project involving Harvard's Project Zero, the Educational Testing Service, and the teachers in the Pittsburgh Public Schools, Howard documents two years spent putting the PROPEL writing portfolio into practice with two eighth grade middle school classes. She identified a series of phases which students in her classes passed through as they created their portfolios, and in this article she discusses the impact of those phases on the students' development.

Hunt, D. C. (1986, December). Preparing a portfolio. *The Instrumentalist, 41,* 30-38.

Hunt discusses how a professional portfolio can be an invaluable asset during a job interview. In this capacity a portfolio can provide evidence of background and experience and can help document answers to questions. Hunt provides suggestions for materials to be included and discusses presentation of the portfolio during an interview.

Johns, J. L. & VanLeirsburg, P. (1990). *Portfolio assessment: A survey among professionals.* Literacy research and reports, Northern Illinois University.

The authors report a survey of 128 educators with regard to their views of assessment, knowledge of portfolios and concerns regarding portfolio assessment. At the time of the survey (June 1990) the majority of educators agreed with the assumptions underlying the portfolio concept, but they knew very little about the use of portfolios. Those educators who had knowledge of portfolios expressed a concern with making decisions about which data documents might be included.

Jongsma, K. S. (1989). Portfolio assessment. *The Reading Teacher, 43* (3), 264-5.

This Question and Answer column focuses on portfolio assessment, with responses from researchers and teachers. In particular, Roger Farr's response is an excellent summary of some of the major issues around the use of portfolios, e.g. guidelines, selection, conferences with students, and so forth.

Levi, R. (1990). Assessment and educational vision: Engaging learners and parents. *Language Arts, 67* (3), 269-273.

Using the work of his students, and the words of the students' parents, Levi documents how portfolios involve students, parents, and teachers as collaborators in the assessment process. He suggests that the portfolio, based on Gardner's contextual approach to assessment, provides a framework for learning, a tool for self-assessment, and a format for collaboration that can encourage students to reach their goals.

Mathews, J. K. (1990). From computer management to portfolio assessment. *The Reading Teacher, 43* (6), 420-1.

As the Orange County, Florida, school district began to view reading and writing as dynamic interactive processes rather than a set of discrete skills, it became apparent that its assessment system must also change to reflect the nature of instruction. In this article Mathews details the steps taken and challenges faced as the district begins to move its elementary schools to a portfolio approach to literacy assessment.

Mills, R. P. (December, 1989). Portfolios capture rich array of student performance. *The School Administrator*, 8-11.

As Vermont's Commissioner of Education, Mills provides an overview of Vermont's struggle to develop a statewide measure of educational performance. The article also previews the new approach developed by the state that will use portfolios as well as standardized tests as tools for the assessment of student performance in writing and math. Mills reviews the procedures for completion as well as assessment of the portfolios and discusses the methods under consideration for public reporting of the results of the assessment process.

Murphy, S. (1990). *Portfolio assessment: Models and variations in the United States.* Paper presented at the annual meeting of the International Reading Association, Atlanta, GA

The author describes various portfolio approaches as a means of detailing the dimensions along which they vary, and define the various approaches: Who makes the assessment decisions? What are the purposes? Who selects what goes into the portfolio? What goes into the portfolio? How much is included? What is done with the portfolio? Who hears about the results? What provisions can be made for revising the portfolio?

Murphy, S. & Smith, M.A. (1990). Talking about portfolios. *The Quarterly 12* (2).

Believing that portfolios can take many forms and that there is no one right way to develop a portfolio, Murphy and Smith suggest that teachers' decisions regarding expectations of the portfolios will have a profound effect on the resulting format and implementation. As examples they cite three schools in California that, as a result of different needs, established quite different portfolio projects. In one school teachers were interested in how students' writing changed with audience and purpose; in another teachers were attempting to tie teaching practices to the motivation of student writers; and in the third portfolios were used to help assess curriculum and student growth. Murphy and Smith discuss the individual programs and document important lessons learned about the use and development of portfolios.

Ogle, D. (1990). *Portfolio assessment: Monitoring teacher change through oral and written components.* Paper presented at the National Reading Conference, Miami, FL.

This paper presents case studies of teachers involved in developing portfolios in terms of their shifts in thinking and teaching practice and discusses the use of portfolios to these ends.

Ohlhausen, M. M. & Ford, M. P. (1990). *Portfolio assessment in teacher education: A tale of two cities.* Paper presented at the National Reading Conference, Miami, FL.
> This study grew out of our belief by the authors (both teacher educators) that teachers enrolled in graduate courses and the students they teach must become responsible for their own learning and evaluation. To this end, they asked: In what ways would portfolio assessment in graduate literacy learning affect teachers and, in turn, these experiences alter the teaching and assessment practices of these teachers in their own classrooms?

Reif, L. (1990). Finding the value in evaluation: Self-assessment in a middle school classroom. *Educational Leadership, 47* (6), 24-29.
> Reif presents a portrait of how portfolios are used in her seventh and eighth grade middle school classes in Durham, New Hampshire, by highlighting the portfolio of one of her students. In her classes "portfolios have become each student's story of who they are as readers and writers." Portfolios are a collection of her students' best work and are used for evaluation by students and teachers. Reif also provides valuable suggestions for providing a supportive classroom environment that promotes the use of portfolios as a tool for assessment.

Roettger, D. & Vavrus, L. (1990). *Evaluating a staff model for implementing student assessment portfolios.* Paper presented at National Reading Conference, Miami, FL.
> Report findings from a project that involves a year-long staff development and research effort in which teachers from selected school districts in Iowa initiate the use of portfolios to assess student literacy learning.

Rynkofs, J. T. (1988). Send your writing folders home. In T. Newkirk and N. Atwell. (Eds.), Understanding writing: Ways of observing, learning, and teaching (2nd ed.), pp. 236-224. Portsmouth, NH: Heinemann.
> Rynkofs states that while the writing folder serves as an important tool for documenting students' growth in written literacy, parents will need help in understanding the development of a child's writing. He, therefore, suggests that folders be sent home with a form that discusses, using written narrative, four important components of the writing folder—"themes the child explored, focus of writing the child used, language and structures the child used, and the mechanics of writing the child learned."

Seidel, S. (1989). Even before portfolios...The activities and atmosphere of a portfolio classroom. *Portfolio, 1* (5) 6-11.
> Seidel, a drama teacher with the Arts PROPEL project, discusses the six ways PROPEL researchers have identified for teachers to bring students into the assessment process, an essential component in the use of portfolios. Opportunities include "providing a number of writing opportunities in a new genre, investigating already accomplished work in the area, collaborating with peers, sharing work, assessment of one's own work, and revision." As Seidel suggests, these opportunities place the student in the center of the assessment process and encourage them to focus on their own learning.

Simmons, J. (1990). Portfolios as large-scale assessment. *Language Arts, 67* (3), 262-267.
> Based on the work done by his research team in Durham, New Hampshire, Simmons discusses a field-test of a large-scale model of portfolio assessment involving portfolios collected randomly to represent the district's entire fifth grade. The researchers compared papers from portfolios with holistically scored timed tests and found that,

unlike a one-shot test, portfolios produced profiles of student writers. They also found that while timed tests and portfolio assessments produced the same rank ordering of students, the portfolios more accurately represented the true abilities of all students. A continuation of the work by the Seacoast Educational Services in the spring of 1990 should add additional insight to what Simmons suggests is a successful combination of large-scale assessment with classroom practice.

Valencia, S. (1990). A portfolio approach to classroom reading assessment: The whys, whats, and hows. *The Reading Teacher, 43* (4), 338-340.

> Based on the assumption that portfolios represent a philosophy that views assessment as an important part of the learning process, this article highlights the research and instructional practices that make portfolios a viable form of assessment. The article also suggests how a portfolio might be organized and implemented in an instructional setting.

Vavrus, L. G. (1989). *Portfolios as alternatives to traditional teacher assessment.* Paper presented at the annual meeting of the National Reading Conference, Austin, TX.

> This paper reports on Stanford University's Teacher Assessment Project's study of performance portfolios as a method of teacher assessment in elementary literacy instruction. Based on concerns resulting from prior applications of portfolios for teacher assessment, the Project developed and piloted portfolios designed to document the daily practice of the teaching of reading and writing. Vavrus provides an interesting discussion of the results of the study and suggests that portfolios can serve as a viable component in a multifaceted assessment program.

Vavrus, L. (1990). Put portfolios to the test. *Instructor, 100* (1), 48-53.

> Vavrus introduces the concept of portfolios and outlines several ideas for teachers to consider, including selection of work to go into portfolios, evaluation, and passing portfolios on to other teachers, however, the article neglects the importance of developing portfolio processes in conjunction with students. The article does include a side-bar interview with Grant Wiggins.

Vavrus, L. G., Athanases, S., Chin, E., Wolf, K., Sugarman, J., & Calfee, R. (1988). *Portfolio development handbook for teachers of elementary literacy.* Technical Report L05, Teacher Assessment Project, Stanford University.

> The authors describe the Stanford Teacher Assessment project in which portfolios are used as a basis for documenting teaching practices and using this documentation to evaluate teachers for certification purposes.

Vavrus, L. G. & Collins, A. (1988) *Portfolio documentation and assessment center exercises: A marriage made for teacher assessment.* Paper presented at the annual meeting of the American Educational Research Association, San Francisco, CA.

> Having developed assessment center exercises and portfolio documentation activities as alternative modes of performance-based assessment for teachers, Stanford University's Teacher Assessment Project is investigating what they term a marriage between the two methods of assessment. In this paper the authors present their plans for a third alternative, the combination of portfolios and assessment center exercises. Vavrus and Collins document the plans as they impact work in elementary literacy and high school biology and discuss the benefits of this combined approach.

Vavrus, L. G. & Calfee, R.C. (1988) *A research strategy for assessing teachers of elementary literacy: The promise of performance portfolios.* Paper presented at the annual meeting of the National Reading Conference, Tuscon, AZ.
> The authors review the development by Stanford University's Teacher Assessment Project of a literacy prototype performance-based assessment for teachers. They provide an overview of the research and highlight the conceptual framework and development of the elementary literacy prototype. Also mentioned are several issues remaining to be addressed, including the nature and use of performance portfolios as a viable method of assessing teacher performance.

Whittier, S. A. (1989). Portfolio reflections: Personalizing education with portfolios. *Portfolio, 1* (4), 5-7.
> In this article Whittier, a vocal arts teacher involved with Arts PROPEL, discusses her portfolio work with seventh graders and her realization that portfolios enable her to personalize her approach to her students' learning.

Winner, E. & Rosenblatt, E. (1989). Tracking the effects of the portfolio process: What changes and when? *Portfolio, 1* (5), 21-26.
> Stating that a PROPEL portfolio is a record of process rather than product, Winner and Rosenblatt discuss student reflections of their work, an important component of the portfolio, and cite the importance of focussing on how portfolios are used in the classroom rather than on their contents. Using the students' own words, they suggest that student growth and learning, as a result of the portfolio process, can be documented in terms of "reflection, involvement in long-term projects, self-confidence, and visual awareness."

Wiser, B. & Dorsey, S. (1990). *Alternative assessment in reading and writing: What we're doing and what we'd like to do in Columbus Public Schools.* Paper presented at National Symposium on Alternative Assessment, Bloomington, IN.
> The authors describe the use of portfolios as an assessment tool being implemented in Columbus Public Schools. Their proposal includes the use of analytic scoring procedures to score selected representative writing pieces. Included in the paper is a discussion of other ongoing development and alternative assessment practices. (e.g., primary trait scoring procedures for open-ended responses to reading passages).

Wolf, D. P. (April, 1989). Portfolio assessment: Sampling student work. *Educational Leadership, 46* (7), 35-39.
> Given the importance of a student's ability to learn how to think and self assess, an important goal of the Arts Propel project was to design ways of evaluating a student's thinking across time that allowed the student to become involved in the evaluation process. In this article Wolf discusses in greater detail the development of Propel portfolios as a tool which accomplishes this goal. The article highlights the characteristics of portfolios that enable students to reflect on the process involved in the development of a wide range of their own written work and discusses the impact this form of evaluation has had on the teachers' ability to assess their students and themselves.

Wolf, D. P. (December, 1987/January, 1988). Opening up assessment. *Educational Leadership, 45,* (4), 24-29.
> Using the work done through Arts PROPEL, Wolf discusses the development, by students and teachers of the arts, of holistic and qualitative modes of assessment of students' thinking processes, problem solving, and self-assessment abilities. She focuses on the tools of projects,

portfolios, and reflective interviews and discusses their ability to provide information for students and teachers about students' development and change across time. Wolf suggests that what is applicable to the arts will transfer to all academic areas.

Wolf, K. (1990). *Student portfolios as a window on teacher knowledge of literacy assessment and instruction.* Paper presented at National Reading Conference, Miami, FL.

> This paper reports findings from an in-depth examination of student portfolios submitted by teachers as part of the Stanford Teacher Assessment Project. The student portfolios framed by the teacher's goals, explanations, and reflections provided evidence of the assessment practices and their appropriateness as well as connections between assessment and instruction.

Wolf, K. (1990). *A portfolio approach to assessing student progress in literacy.* Paper presented at the National Reading Conference, Miami, FL.

> This paper reports research on portfolio assessment in literacy and was pursued with two goals in mind: developing an approach to using portfolios and the influence on teachers' instructional decisions and evaluations of their students. The portfolio assessment had two parts: student work (included in writing folders, literative logs, library check-out cards) and teacher records (anecdotal records, observational checklists, surveys, test results, etc.). Over the course of the year, teachers' views of students became more positive and their instruction more tailored to their students.

Zessoules, R. (1989). The dance marathon: learning over time. *Portfolio, 1* (5), 11-19.

> Zessoules looks at the use of portfolios in introductory choreography classes as a tool not only to document what students have learned but also to reveal the processes involved as new skills are discovered. For students in the choreography classes portfolios have become a way of building their own "history as learners," and as a result assessment and learning are integrated. Through examples of student choreographers, Zessoules provides a concrete picture of the students' interaction with their portfolios as they develop understanding of their own growth and development.

Articles, Papers, and Books about Assessment

Afflerbach, P. (1990). *The appropriateness of report cards for communicating teachers' knowledge of student literacy achievement.* Paper presented at 40th Annual meeting of National Reading Conference, Miami, FL.

> Traces studies describing the use of report card, as well as his own analyses of teacher decision-making in conjunction with using different report cards.

Afflerbach, P. (Ed.) (in press). *Issues in statewide reading assessments.* Washington, DC: American Research Institutes.

> Explores a host of assessment related topics of pertinence to assessment and evaluation at various levels.

Atwell, N. Making the grade. In T. Newkirk and N. Atwell. (Eds.), *Understanding writing: Ways of observing, learning, and teaching* (2nd ed.) (pp. 236-244). Portsmouth, NH: Heinemann.

> In this article Atwell discusses the use of conferences to evaluate students' writing. Expecting grades to reflect students' growth in areas

such as topic selection, involvement, language, effort, completeness, and editing, Atwell believes it is essential to discuss with students their accomplishments and goals. Through the use of example, she provides an overview of the procedures used and an explanation of an evaluation conference.

Barrs, M. (1990). The primary language record: reflection of issues in evaluation. *Language Arts, 67* (3), 244-253.
> This article discusses the benefits of the Primary Language Record (PLR), an assessment tool developed by the Inner London Education Authority. Barr briefly discusses several of the strategies incorporated into the observation-based record, including structured observation, samples, error analysis, conferencing, teacher judgment scales and cumulative records. She highlights the value of such assessment techniques as compared to traditional standardized tests and finds that the PLR allows for systematic observation and diagnosis that can immediately impact student learning. As are portfolios, Barrs suggests that the PLR is multidimensional in that it results in observation on a variety of occasions over time and in a variety of contexts and involves a number of different techniques of recording and assessment.

Barrs, M., Ellis, S., Hester, H., & Thomas, A. (1988). *The primary language record*. Portsmouth, NH: Heinemann.
> Developed and piloted as part of an initiative for the Center of Language in Primary Education, this publication is one of the best sources available for implementable ideas related to analyzing reading and writing. Certain principles undergird *The Primary Language Record:* involvement of parents, teachers and children; the importance of rewarding development in all areas of language; a clear framework for evaluating progress in language; and the importance of meeting the needs of people in different language groups.

Bintz, W. & Harste, J. C. (1990). *Whole language and the future of literacy assessment: Some insights and concerns.* Paper presented at the National Symposium on Alternative Assessment in the Language Arts, Indiana University, Bloomington, IN.
> This paper discusses the problems with traditional assessment approaches as well as the advantages and disadvantages of current alternatives such as variations on standardized testing, literacy portfolio approaches, and holistic assessment procedures.

Calfee, R. C. (1987). The school as a context for assessment of literacy. *The Reading Teacher, 40* (8), 738-743.
> In this article Calfee defines assessment as a process of exchanges between teacher and student that involves instruction and assessment as an integral part of the assessment process. He suggests that teacher questioning further enhances this process by providing a chance for immediate assessment of student progress and of program effectiveness and, as a result, enhances the relationship between curriculum, instruction, and assessment.

Calfee, R. & Hiebert, E. (1990). Classroom assessment of reading. In R. Barr, M. L. Kamil, P. Mosenthal & P. D. Pearson (Eds.), *Handbook of Reading Research*, (Vol. 2). White Plains, NY: Longman.
> The authors provide a comprehensive discussion of assessment practices in elementary reading-writing classrooms in which they focus on the nature and outcomes of externally mandated tests and internal assessment (i.e., classroom-based procedures). The chapter closes with thoughts about future directions.

Clay, M. M. (1990). Research currents: What is and what might be in evaluation. *Language Arts, 67* (3), 288-298.

> In this article Clay discusses her view of teaching and evaluation as it is practiced in New Zealand and makes suggestions for its improvement. She suggests that standardized tests serve well as outcome measures but provide little information in terms of how to teach to change the outcomes. A review of current practices in New Zealand elementary schools documents how teachers have developed informal measures that go beyond the standardized tests to evaluate student growth and change. Clay calls for the development of measures at all levels of education that evaluate process and product and reminds us that such methods empower teachers as well as learners.

Farr, R., Lewis, M., Fasholz, J., Pinsky, E., Towle, S., Lipschutz, J., & Faulds, B. P. (March 1990). Writing in response to reading. *Educational Leadership, 47* (6), 66-69.

> Roger Farr explains the development of Writing in Response to Reading, an instructional program covering all grade levels begun in the River Forest School District in Illinois. The program was developed to integrate the use of reading and writing and includes an assessment component that allows assessment to match and measure instruction. Teachers were involved in the development and testing of the rubric so that assessment is consistent across grade levels and allows the district to measure student progress. The result is a district that is more comfortably moving away from assessment of isolated practices to more holistic scoring of reading and writing.

Farr, R. & Carey, R. F. (1986). *Reading: What can be measured?* (2nd edition). Newark, DE: International Reading Association.

> This second edition represents one of the most comprehensive and critical reviews of assessment issues in reading.

Frederiksen, J. R. & Collins, A. (1989). A systems approach to educational testing. *Educational Researcher, 18* (9), 27-32.

> Frederiksen and Collins argue for the systemic validity of tests. This extension of the notion of validity is important for it takes into account the effects of instructional changes brought about by the introduction of the test into an educational system.

Goodman, K. S., Goodman, Y. M., & Hood, W. J. (1989). *The whole language evaluation book*. Portsmouth, NH: Heinemann.

> The authors describe various attempts by teachers to develop assessment procedures in line with classroom practices; portfolios are among those discussed.

Jett-Simpson, M., Dauer, V., Dussault, N. Gaulke, B., Gerhart, L., Leslie, L., McClain-Ruell, L., Pinlott, J., Prentice, W., & Telfer, R. (1990). *Toward an ecological assessment of reading*. Madison, WI: Wisconsin State Reading Association.

> As stated in their introduction "Ecological assessment is assessment that transcends informal classroom assessment." Grounded in the relationship of readers to their reading environment, it is systematic planned assessment of students' reading behaviors in classroom settings where they are engaged in authentic reading tasks with authentic texts. This monograph provides a thoughtful discussion in the problems of traditional assessment on the way to suggesting guidelines and describing a host of practices (book selection, observation, response journals, think-alouds, interviews, portfolios) that might be used by classroom teachers.

Johnston, P. (1989). Steps toward a more naturalistic approach to the assessment of the reading process. In J. Algina & S. Legg (Eds.),

Cognitive assessment of language and mathematics outcomes. Norwood, NJ: Ablex.

> This chapter provides a rationale and some guidelines for a naturalistic approach to assessment—that is, observations of children's performances as these behaviors occur.

Johnston, P. (1987). Assessing the process, and the process of assessment in the language arts. *The Dynamics of Language Learning.* Urbana, IL: NCTE.

> This article provides an excellent argument for process assessment in the language arts. Johnston suggests there are three characteristics important for effective assessment: "the information collected is useful and is used in a timely manner, the procedure for collection is efficient, and the information provided is of high quality." He also highlights the differences between measurement and evaluation, suggesting there is little use for measurement in the educational process since it is not "action-oriented" and the attributes measured are often questionable. He, therefore, recommends assessment processes that are "well-developed, independently motivated, self-correcting, and stress the importance of motivation."

Johnston, P. (1987). Teachers as evaluation experts. *The Reading Teacher, 40* (8), 744-748.

> Johnston discusses how teachers can most effectively evaluate the process of literacy development by suggesting they become experts at "detecting patterns, knowing classroom procedures, and by listening." He further suggests that such individualized process centered evaluation not only serves instruction but also allows students and teachers to collaborate in the learning process.

Johnston, P. (1984). Assessment in reading. In P. D. Pearson, R. Barr, M. L. Kamil, & P. Mosenthal (Eds.) *Handbook of research in reading.* (Vol. 1). New York: Longman.

> The author offers a comprehensive examination of assessment issues, including suggesting several challenges for the future.

Krest, M. (1987). Time on my hands: Handling the paper load. *English Journal, 76* (8), 37-42.

> Krest argues that the teaching and grading of writing must reflect a sound research-based theory and suggests that since growth in writing is developmental, it is important for teachers to approach the task of assessment as responsive adults guiding students to recognize their own strengths and weaknesses. She provides numerous techniques to assist in the process, including the use of the portfolio as a guide to assessment. She suggests that portfolios be collected quarterly and that they contain drafts and revisions, as well as final products of four pieces. Students determine the one piece in each portfolio that will be specifically graded, and grades reflect efforts at revision as well as the success or failure of the final product.

Lucas, C. K. (1988). Toward ecological evaluation, Part 1. *The Quarterly, 10* (1), 1-3, 12-17.

> Lucas suggests a move beyond tests that are worth teaching toward an ecological model of evaluation. Such a model includes tests that "reflect the whole writing environment of the learner and impacts that environment in positive rather than negative ways." In Part I of this article she highlights the history of writing assessment prior to her suggested reforms by dividing that history into three parts. Phase I includes direct measures of writing assessment; Phase II, the introduction of the essay tests in response to criticism of direct measures; and Phase III, the move toward creating "tests worth teaching to." Lucas suggests that current

experimentation with portfolios is a recognition of the need to go beyond Phase III toward a new model of evaluation.

Lucas, C. K. (1988). Toward ecological evaluation, Part 2. *The Quarterly, 10* (2), 4-10.

In the second part of this article Lucas describes in detail Phase IV assessment, which she suggests is based on "literacy performance fully contextualized in the classroom." This phase adds a new dimension to ecological evaluation by providing assessment that increases the "amount, quantity, and usefulness" of the information provided by assessment to the teachers and students. Lucas suggests that assessment becomes part of the context of the classroom, so that assessment can reflect what is naturally occurring in the class.

Pearson, P. D. & Valencia, S. (1987). Assessment, accountability and professional prerogative. In J. E. Readence & R. S. Baldwin. (Eds.), *Research in literacy: Merging perspectives.* 36th yearbook of the National Reading Conference. Rochester, NY: National Reading Conference.

The authors explore a wide range of assessment issues in terms of the relationship between new assessment alternatives and issues of accountability, especially at the state level.

Pikulski, J. J. (1989). The assessment of reading: A time for change? *The Reading Teacher, 43* (1), 80-81.

In this October 1989 article reviewing the state of assessment in reading, Pikulski discusses what the readers of *The Reading Teacher* can expect to find in the assessment column during the 1989-90 year. He suggests that an important concept being discussed in the field is the portfolio approach to the assessment of reading and literacy, and highlights the potential of portfolios for placing teachers and learners at the center of the assessment process.

Routman, R. (1991). *Invitations: Changing as Teacher and Learners, K-12.* Portsmouth, NH: Heinemann.

The author includes a rich description of classroom assessment and evaluation practices for teachers making the transition toward more naturalistic and student-empowering assessment.

Shepard, L. A. (1989). Why we need better assessments. *Educational Leadership, 46* (7), 4-9.

The large-scale use and limitations of standardized tests are discussed, and the separation of such accountability measures from those that inform instruction is suggested. Problems facing the construction of such accountability tests are noted, and the resulting practices of teaching to the test are discussed. It is suggested that better instructional assessment needs to be developed that allows assessment to resemble learning tasks and involves the development of portfolios that contain samples of students' work. It is also suggested that such a strong difference exists between accountability and instructional assessment that the two cannot be merged. Finally, the article suggests the use of scientific samples to enhance the credibility of standardized tests.

Stayter, F. Z. & Johnston, P. (1990). Evaluating the teaching and learning of literacy. In T. Shanahan (Ed.), *Reading and writing together: New perspectives for the classroom.* (pp. 253-271). Norwood, MA: Christopher-Gordon.

Stayter and Johnston discuss the integration of reading, writing, teaching, and learning and suggest that evaluation needs to be an integral component of this process. Believing that evaluation is constructive, they look at the impact that techniques, focus, and language have on evaluation of learners, as well as at the importance of the context in which learning occurs, and at the opportunities students are given for self-assessment. Several tools for evaluation are discussed, including portfolios, interviewing, student questioning, and teacher evaluation.

Taylor, D. (1990). Teaching without testing. *English Education*, 22 (1), 4-74.

Taylor presents the essence of a project intent on developing biographic literacy profiles from the perspective of the child. She provides a rich description of the features and methods associated with the various objectives of the project: Learning to Observe Children's Literacy Behaviors; Learning to Develop Note-taking Procedures to Record Observations of Children Reading and Writing; Learning to Write Descriptive Biographic Literacy Profiles; and Learning to Increase our Awareness of the Multiple Layers of Interpretation that We Are Incorporating into the Children's Biographic Literacy Profiles.

Tierney, R. J. & McGinley, W. (In press). Serious flaws in written literacy assessment. In A. Carrasquillo and C. Hedley (Eds.), *Whole language and the bilingual learner*. Norwood, NJ: Ablex.

Explores in some detail the limitations (especially mismatch between what is literacy and how it is taught versus testing practice) of standardized testing practices that are mandated.

Valencia, S. & Pearson, P. D. (1987). Reading assessment: Time for a change. *The Reading Teacher*, 40. (8), 726-732.

In this article Valencia and Pearson claim that the current view of reading that emphasizes the active role of readers as they construct meaning with a text is not reflected in our present practices. By presenting the pilot projects begun in Illinois to develop new statewide assessment measures, they document the need for developing a new framework for thinking about assessment that is based on our current knowledge of the reading process and considers the decision-making levels of our educational system.

Valencia, S. W. & Pearson, P. D. (1990). *National survey of the use of test data for educational decision-making*. Reading Research and Education Center Technical Report, University of Illinois at Urbana-Champaign.

This report describes the scope and nature of testing—especially reading testing—and how different tests are selected and used by teachers and administrators. Above all, the report provides systematic data bearing on how tests influence educational decision-making and teaching.

Valencia, S.W., McGinley, W. & Pearson, P. D. (1990). Assessing reading and writing. In G. Duffy (Ed.), *Reading in the middle school.* (pp. 124-153). Newark, DE: International Reading Association.

The authors advocate a move to contextualized assessment that views assessment as "continuous, multidimensional, grounded in knowledge, and authentic" and suggest that portfolios in their philosophical sense reflect a dynamic attitude toward assessment that integrates instruction and assessment. However, believing that teachers need criteria for evaluating their own assessment strategies, they offer a set of five continua for evaluation of assessment strategies—"focus, structure, mode, locus of control, and intrusiveness"—and provide scenarios to serve as conceptual frameworks in the analysis process.

Wiggins, G. (1989). Teaching to the (authentic) test. *Educational Leadership*, 46 (7), 41-47.

As Wiggins argues, "If tests determine what teachers teach and what students will study for—and they do—then the road to reform is a straight but steep one." The problem as Wiggins states it is for tests to be authentic, (i.e., truly representative of performance in the field), tied to criteria that make sense; involve student self-assessment, and so on.

References

Apple, M.W. (1986). *Teacher and texts.* Boston: Routledge and Kegan Paul.

Athanases, S. Z. (1990). Assessing the planning and teaching of integrated language arts in the elementary grades. Report L3. Teacher Assessment Project, CERAS 507, School of Education, Stanford University, Stanford, CA 94305-3084. Lee S. Shulman, Principal Investigator.

Associated Press (May 3, 1989). Students subvert own scores. *New York Times Education.*

Cronbach, L.J. (1971). Test validation. In R.L. Thorndike (Ed.), *Educational Measurement* (pp. 443-507). Washington, D.C.: American Council on Education.

Freire, P. (1970). *Pedagogy of the oppressed.* New York: Seabury.

Freire, P. (1978). *Pedagogy in process.* New York: Seabury.

McGinley, W.J. & Madigan, D. (1990). *Linking literacy and social change: A study of fourth grade writers in an urban elementary school.* Paper presented at the National Reading Conference 40th Annual Meeting, Miami, FL.

Ogbu, J.U. (1983). Literacy and schooling in subordinate cultures: The case of Black Americans. In D. Resnick (Ed.) *Literacy in historical perspective.* Washington, DC: Library of Congress.

Shor, I. (1986). *Cultural wars: School and society in the conservative restoration.* Boston: Routledge and Kegan Paul.

Wigginton E. (1975). *The foxfire books.* (Vols. 1-3). New York: Doubleday.

Index